Praise for *The Defiant Optimist*

"An inspiring read by a passionate trailblazer. Durreen Shahnaz shares her remarkable experiences challenging the status quo, beating the odds, and fueling change."
—**Adam Grant**, #1 *New York Times* bestselling author of *Think Again* and host of the TED podcast *Re: Thinking*

"Read *The Defiant Optimist* and be inspired to make your journey of inclusion and sustainability! This is the silver lining to the challenging climate we live in today, whether in terms of the environment, our culture, or the economy. It is a reminder that within all of us, there is a defiant optimist who can make a change. Through Shahnaz's captivating stories and deep insights, this book becomes the firestarter we never knew we needed. As a woman entrepreneur committed to sustainable and responsible growth, I applaud her vision, mission, and courage."
—**Claire Chiang**, co-founder of Banyan Tree Holdings

"As the world pushes for gender equality and women's representation in the global financial system, Durreen Shahnaz is one of the few who has rolled up her sleeves and done the work of lifting women up. With its compelling and intricate details, this book demonstrates the spirit of the defiant optimist with which Shanaz changes a system that works only for the 1 percent. It is timely, necessary, and most importantly, empowering for all who want to create change, however small."
—**Professor Muhammad Yunus**, founder of Grameen Bank and Nobel Peace Prize winner

"Durreen Shahnaz details her boundary-pushing experiences with candor, wisdom, and vivid storytelling. Documenting her journey from war-torn Bangladesh to the pinnacle of the financial markets, Shahnaz reveals the importance of finance in sustainable development and women's empowerment. Her passion flows through *The Defiant Optimist*, inspiring women and girls and reminding them of the power they hold if they only dare to dream. She is a wonderful role model for girls and women everywhere."

—**Dr. Judith Rodin**, former president of the Rockefeller Foundation and former president of the University of Pennsylvania

"This book is a rare window into what impact investing really means on the ground, bridging the back streets and the Wall Streets of the world. Few are armed with the tenacity of Durreen Shahnaz, and even fewer go on to chart exceptional paths in creating impact for those the financial system leaves behind. This book reminds us that a revolutionary change starts from a small step. Let that step be *The Defiant Optimist*, and it will inspire you for miles to come."

—**Antony Bugg-Levine**, co-founder of the Global Impact Investment Network

"Durreen Shahnaz's poignant account of her life's journey, especially the courageous steps she has taken on her career path, highlights three key lessons: promoting women's education and empowerment; advancing diversity, equity, and inclusion; and summoning the courage to identify sources of power. This memoir will inspire readers to embrace what Shahnaz calls the 'defiant optimist' mindset as they strive to create better futures for themselves and for the world."

—**Kathleen McCartney**, president of Smith College

"Few in the field of global impact investing have been as steadfast and engaged in advancing a vision of finance with justice as Durreen Shahnaz. The opportunity to learn from her journey and lessons in activism and financial innovation is not to be missed!"

—**Jed Emerson**, Global Lead of Impact Investing at Tiedemann Advisors

The
DEFIANT
OPTIMIST

DARING TO FIGHT GLOBAL INEQUALITY,
REINVENT FINANCE, AND INVEST IN WOMEN

The
DEFIANT
OPTIMIST

Durreen Shahnaz

Broadleaf Books
Minneapolis

THE DEFIANT OPTIMIST
Daring to Fight Global Inequality, Reinvent Finance, and Invest in Women

Lines from the unpublished poem "I Was Born into a Body" by Sadaf Saaz are used with the permission of the author.

Some names have been changed to protect the identity or privacy of individuals in this book.

Cover image: Getty Images/Nataleana
Cover design: Olga Grlic

Print ISBN: 978-1-5064-8076-3
eBook ISBN: 978-1-5064-8077-0

Printed in Canada

To Bubu and Ma, for sowing the seeds of defiance.
To Diya and Aliya, for giving me countless reasons to be optimistic.

I was born into a body
that now walks tall
Taking its place in the world
with a stride that is bold
Beautiful in its defiance
Unabashed
Unashamed

I was born into a body
which now has a voice.

—Sadaf Saaz
Bangladeshi Writer and Poet

Contents

CONTENTS

PART IV: IMAGINE A NEW WORLD

PART V: CREATE YOUR OWN CHANGE

Preface

In the evenings when I was young, my grandmother stitched blankets out of old saris. These cotton saris, worn by the women in my family as they worked, had become worn and thin. But stitched together with intricate *nakshi* (designs), the saris were reborn as *kantha*: blankets, which would keep us warm at night.

With the fabric spread across the bed, my grandmother would stoop over and patiently stitch beautiful patterns—sun, moon, stars, flowers, and leaves—with multicolor threads. Using traditional Bengali quilting stitches that women in the villages used to sew layers of saris together, she bent close to the fabric, embroidering elaborate and beautiful motifs. When her sister and nieces visited, they, too, along with my mother and grandmother, would sit on the bed, legs crossed, and join in stitching. They talked while they worked, catching up on each other's lives. I watched, marveling both at the intricacy of their designs and the bond between them.

Years later, working in microfinance in Bangladesh, I watched rural women stitch nakshi kantha just like my grandmother and aunts did. I often walked into a courtyard surrounded by mud huts and banana trees to find a group of women stitching kanthas as chickens ran around their ankles. Chewing betel nut and tobacco leaves, the women shared stories of sorrow and hope as they worked.

Each kantha, an elaborate art of blessings and empowerment, would be given to another woman in the community. The more elaborate kanthas were often gifts for brides-to-be. Whenever I asked about the story behind a particular nakshi, or design, the women would blush and giggle. Then the needleworker who had designed the blanket would pull the end of the sari that covered her head a little tighter, perhaps to give herself the confidence to speak up.

The nakshi represented her own unfulfilled hopes, she said quietly, so that the new bride could fulfill them. The design of a boat represented the travels the needleworker had longed to take but for which she never had the opportunity. Two birds kissing symbolized the true and tender love of a husband that she longed for. An open book represented the education that she wanted but could not obtain, and the rice field stood for the abundant crop that was beyond her reach because she did not own any land.

Spread before us, the faded colors of the saris came alive with the unfulfilled dreams and aspirations of the needleworkers. I would sit on the ground with these women, on mats woven from dry palm leaves, and look around the circle in wonder. They wanted to feed themselves and their families, to educate their children, and to make beautiful things that last.

Their kanthas contained messages. These blankets, and the designs they carried, passed on the longing that a young woman would find opportunities and blessings the needleworker herself had never had. Written on beloved and worn saris, those designs became dispatches of defiant hope.

***

Economic inequality. Environmental collapse. Gender injustice. Pandemic. War. The fundamental ills of this world remain the same over centuries. These things haunted our grandparents and great-grandparents, and they remain top of mind for us today.

More than 2 billion people are living under $1.25 a day, and they live by oceans that are swelling and forests that are burning. The COVID-19 pandemic has exacerbated the wealth gap and the gender gap, with women across the world bearing the brunt of economic and social upheaval.

Meanwhile, wealth and power are burgeoning—concentrated among a small group of people. The top 1 percent of households globally own 43 percent of all personal wealth, while the bottom 50 percent own only 1 percent. The world today has more than three thousand billionaires. Our global financial system is worth over $160 trillion—and it is managed, maneuvered, and manipulated by 1 percent of the population. In 2019, the world's billionaires held more wealth than 4.6 billion people.

In this system, women, minorities, and residents of the Global South are categorically excluded from the table, especially within financial markets. Globally, women still earn only 77 cents on each dollar that men earn. Close to 2 billion women from the Global South barely appear either as major investors or investees in the all-powerful global financial markets. A just world will remain a fantasy until they do.

This book tells the story of my journey to ensure that financial markets hear the voices of women and represent the concerns of people of color and underserved communities. It's a story of challenging Wall Street to change its definition of risk and redefine value to uplift work that creates good in this world.

This journey to shape finance for good has been a long one. First, I had to understand the system; then, over decades, I had to find ways to repurpose it and make it inclusive of social justice. Along the way I discovered the power of what I have come to call *defiant optimism*: the stubbornly hopeful refusal to accept what others might call "fate" or "just the way things are."

Defiant optimism is what I saw among the women stitching nakshi kantha in Bangladesh: the audacity to believe that women deserve education and the chance to determine their own futures. It is the relentless determination to change the way the world works and the resilient optimism that such change is possible. It's the stubborn belief that systems that benefit the few can be transformed for the good of the many.

It's the attitude I've seen modeled by women I've met with around the globe, in places like Cambodia, Egypt, India, Indonesia, Jordan, the Philippines, and Guatemala—women who refuse to accept that what they've been told is their fate is the same as their future. Women who stitch their own unrealized dreams into empowerment for others, and who defy common wisdom enough to imagine a different world into being.

You can be a defiant optimist, no matter what work you do. Public sector, private sector, or anything in between: what if people across all industries committed to expanding structures of power and access to those who have been denied? What if we all together became defiant optimists? Could we dare to imagine a world where we break down walls and fight to heal the planet's ills?

A defiant optimist needs the practical chops to build a realistic pathway for herself and others to join her. So in these pages I share what I have learned and invite you to join me on this path.

Voices are shouting from the tin rooftops of the Global South, fighting against all those who work to hold us down and shove solutions down our throats. This is the story of a defiant girl rising up, seeking the sources of power, and finding the optimism to fuel change. It's the story of defiant optimists across the globe who are stitching threads of defiance and hope and dreams of a better future. It can be your story too.

PART I

Stitch Threads of Defiance

CHAPTER ONE

Being a Girl

In my mother's eyes, I never should have happened. On every birthday, dating back as far as I can recall, Ma would remind me that my gender had been a cruel mistake. "You were supposed to be a *boy!*" she'd lament, wringing her hands, as if willing me to be replaced by a male heir. "You kicked around so much. I could feel you were going to be a boy!"

Each year on my birthday, my maternal grandfather Dadu would pull me aside. He dabbled in astrology as a hobby, and he had logged the exact time I was born: year, month, day, and time. "According to the astrological charts, the moment you were born comes just once in a century," he'd say, pausing for effect, his eyebrows raised and his voice somber. "The moment is called *chura moni: chura*, the peak; *moni*, the jewel. When a boy child is born at the very time that you were born, the universe ensures that he will reach great heights."

At this point in the story, which I heard many times before, I always hoped the ending would be different. I longed that Dadu's reading of my fate this time would dictate that I, a girl child, would reach great heights too. I wanted assurance that this historic and once-in-a-century moment of fortunate birth, chura moni, could include me.

But the story always ended the same way. "But alas, the moment of chura moni was wasted on you," Dadu would say sadly. "You were born a girl."

To understand my mother's and grandfather's dismay, you need to understand my family. You need to understand the land of my birth, Bangladesh, and Bengali culture. I was born in Dhaka, now the capital of Bangladesh, the fourth daughter of a mother whose very happiness depended on the gender of her children. Three sisters had come before me. First, came Mahreen in the late 1950s. As the first child, she was my parents' favorite. Then came Sharmeen in the early 1960s. She was bright, with a photographic memory but always sickly. A few years later came Tazneen: the most feminine, beautiful, and delicate of us all. And then came me. In the brief span of a decade, my mother gave birth to four girls.

It wasn't unusual for a woman in our society to pin her hopes on producing sons. Many cultures still reward women who bear male offspring. Gender bias, specifically preference for sons, means that globally there are about 1.5 million missing female births every year due to sex-selective abortions. This phenomenon is most acute in Asia, especially in China and South Asia. Patriarchal values across many countries still tend to give men and boys incredible advantages and control over opportunities and resources, and factors like gender-based violence, unequal access to schooling, and child marriage harm girls and women.

So in the time and culture in which I grew up, a wife's greatest responsibility—some might argue her *only* responsibility—was to produce male offspring. If she were lucky enough to give birth to a boy early in the marriage, she could move on to other things. But if she failed—if, like my mother, she produced four girls in a row—her value as a wife, as a person, remained in question.

Ma had a traditional arranged marriage to Papa when she was nineteen. Papa was twenty-six. Keeping to conservative Muslim tradition, my parents were in separate rooms during their wedding ceremony. They had not met before the ceremony, and this custom ensured that they would not meet during the ceremony either. Nevertheless, both my parents answered yes three times when asked by the imam if they would take the other person as a life partner. They were already husband and wife when they met each other, for the first time, on their wedding night.

They were a mismatch from the very beginning, but neither wanted to admit it. They had too much to lose. Their union was a practical one, designed to benefit the extended family. Papa was an academic on track for a promising career in government. He came from no money but had a well-known family title and smarts galore. Papa loved his books, doing crosswords, and playing chess. His mother, who arranged the marriage, saw in Ma a means to improve the family's lot in life. That stemmed not only from the reputation and wealth of my mother's family but also from her beauty.

Without question, Ma was beautiful. With lush dark hair, big brown eyes, flawless skin, and an enviable figure, my mother was like a Bengali Daisy Buchanan, the charming heroine in F. Scott Fitzgerald's *The Great Gatsby*. Draped in a beautiful sari, Ma could hold court and cast a spell on all men and women who met her. Ma could also pick up languages effortlessly. She was fluent in Bengali, English, Urdu, Sanskrit, and Hindi. She could speak more dialects than I could count on my fingers and knew a smattering of French and Persian. She loved to socialize. At dinner parties, she was the flame around which guests gathered, charming people with her jokes, puns, and stories and fluidly moving from one language to another.

Ma longed for her life to include traveling, watching movies, and socializing. But because Papa's family was not well off, and he was the eldest son, he sent most of the meager salary he earned as a civil servant to his family to support his parents, eight sisters, and two brothers. My parents lived with my mother's parents, who in turn supported them. And without any other sources of money in the family, this is the way their lives would always be.

So when I entered the world, I wasn't just a source of disappointment, I was a constant reminder to my mother of her inadequacy. As a little girl, I had to wrap my mind around this heavy truth: I was the emblem of my mother's failure, as a woman, to deliver.

***

My maternal grandmother, whom we called Bubu, married my grandfather through an arranged marriage when she was just eleven years old. Back then this was not uncommon, and it was hardly taboo. No one would have thought of her as a child bride; she was simply a bride. At the time of marriage, Dadu was seventeen and considered a man.

For Bubu, marriage at eleven was a way of life in which she had no say. Even one hundred years after my grandmother's marriage, according to the United Nations (UN), South Asia still has the highest rate of child marriage in the world, and Bangladesh has the highest rate in Asia. Close to half the women in the region are still married before the age of eighteen, and nearly one in five are younger than fifteen. These child marriages put girls at high risk of exploitation, violence, and abuse. In the blink of an eye, a child bride like Bubu goes from being her father's property to her husband's, and she is often used as a negotiation tool among families.

As my grandmother was relatively dark-skinned, she was considered unattractive and potentially not marriageable. To overcome this, her father used the promise of foreign education for the potential groom as a bargaining chip. After the wedding, however, Bubu's family reneged on this deal. Dadu never forgave Bubu for this, although she had had no voice in any part of this transaction.

Not that a lack of a foreign education held Dadu back. He attended one of the top universities in British India on scholarship, earned his law degree, and went on to become a prominent judge in the Indian state of East Bengal under the British Raj, or colonial rule. Meanwhile, his young wife remained in her village home, led a quiet, pious life, took care of her family, and never received a formal education. Bubu's learning was limited to signing her name and reading some Bengali with much difficulty. Years later, when I was teaching women in rural villages to sign their names to receive the first loan of their lives, I would see Bubu's smile on each of their faces as they beamed with newly acquired power. With one signature came a measure of freedom.

Once Dadu returned from Calcutta and joined the judicial service, Bubu's existence revolved around taking care of him and setting up a home wherever Dadu's position took them. Over the decades, it was her job to clean and fold his clothes. It was her job to prepare the foods he liked and to make certain that his yogurt was just the right consistency. And it was her job to clean and polish Dadu's hookah, the three-foot-high water pipe with a brass base.

But never—no matter how faithfully she cooked and cleaned for Dadu—could she bring herself to look into his eyes. And never could she call him by his name. For as long as I can recall, my grandmother referred to my grandfather, the father of her only daughter, in formal terms, as Joj Shahib, or Mr. Judge. It was as if she had never shared a bed with the man, as if she lived in awe and perhaps even fear of him.

Yet the kitchen was her domain. Bubu would sit on the floor and grind spices with *shil patta*, the Bengali version of stone mortar and pestle, and spend hours in her garden to find the right ingredients to make *bhorta* (a side dish of mashed herbs, spice seeds, or vegetable paste to be mixed with rice) to spice up our otherwise humble meals. Knowing my love of food, Bubu would indulge me with little treats of bread when I got tired of eating rice. She would heat the bread for me and gently admonish me, "How can you be a good Bengali girl if you don't like rice? When you get married, you will need to cook rice every day. What do you think: you will marry an *engrez shahib* (a white man) and eat potatoes all the time?"

As Bubu watched me drink my milk and eat my bread, she would give a lot of free advice on how to cook a special dish or take care of the fruit trees. Occasionally she would add in some advice on boys and men. "Remember: men are like children," she would say. "They don't understand the ways of the world very well. That is why we women have to take care of them and do the thinking for them. Let them scream and shout. They don't have the power; we do." I would just nod my head.

While Dadu ate his lunch in silence—alone and precisely at 1:00 p.m., per his Ayurvedic practice—Bubu would stand and serve him, anticipating his needs. Once Dadu had finished his lunch, smoked his hookah, and retreated to his room for his afternoon nap, the whole household would come to a sleepy, slow, midday rest. Bubu, who took her midday rest after others, waited for this moment.

When it was time for Dadu's after-meal smoke, I would watch as Bubu carefully placed the burning charcoal on the clay tobacco holder. I'd watch as she blew gently and steadily into the clay receptacle to get the tobacco burning at just the right temperature.

I was the only person in the household who did not sleep in the afternoons. It was the perfect time to climb trees, play with my slingshot, or sneak a taste of the various fruit pickles Bubu put in glass jars out in the sun to marinate. But sometimes, before starting my afternoon adventures, I watched as my grandmother transformed into someone else entirely.

Looking around the house and making sure nobody was close by, she would sit next to the hookah in Dadu's chair, a comfortable wicker chair nobody else was allowed to use, on the veranda. She would settle in, take hold of the pipe in one hand, close her eyes, and inhale deeply from the pipe. With that inhale, Bubu changed before my eyes. She would take in the loud burble of air bubbles in the brass water base of the hookah and then languidly open her eyes and let out the smoke, her lips curving into a smile.

Hiding behind a curtain, I wondered at her bravery and defiance. In a society where only men smoked and only the elder men smoked in public, here was Bubu, smiling, nodding, and happily smoking away. Smoking that pipe was, for her, a reclamation of something—an assertion of her right to take up space. There are many ways to be a rebel, she seemed to say.

Observing their marriages, I vowed I would never live like my mother or my grandmother. I did not want an arranged marriage. I did not want to be a child bride. I did not want a disinterested or unloving husband or to be treated as a servant or a trophy wife. I did not want to get respect only when I bore a son.

No. When I grew up, I would neither allow a system to dictate my life nor settle for a false sense of power. I would not be a rebel in secret only. I would inhale joy and independence without worrying about who was looking.

CHAPTER TWO

Tea with Soldiers

My parents, grandparents, siblings, and I lived in a two-story house my grandfather had built on a large plot of land in the middle of Dhaka. It was a white, post–World War II art deco building. The story goes that Dadu did not like the architect, so in the middle of construction, he fired him and redesigned the house himself. While he may have been a brilliant judge, Dadu had no architectural training, so the house had hallways in strange places, windows where there should have been doors, and vice versa.

Dadu rented out the upstairs portion of the house to supplement the family income, while our family resided downstairs. The quarters were close, with three generations confined to three bedrooms. My parents occupied one bedroom, Dadu had another, and we four sisters and Bubu shared the remaining bedroom. I cannot tell you exactly how we made things work, with all five of us crowded together in one small room. None of us had anything to call our own. But we did it, sharing beds and desks and clothes.

Our home boasted lots of fruit trees, which were Bubu's passion, and a beautiful garden, which was Ma's. Ma was crazy about few things more than her garden. For her, gardening was an escape. She won prize after prize for her massive roses and exotic orchids. Those prizes were a small compensation for the many things in life she could not have.

Ma's gardening was just one portion of a greater plan to keep up appearances. Appearances were everything. She wanted society to admire her family like they did her garden. Ma sewed beautiful dresses for us from her saris and knitted and crocheted gorgeous cardigans and shawls. She taught us how to create Japanese flower arrangements to decorate the living room. In her mind, we had to know how to create beauty in case we weren't beautiful enough ourselves to attract attention. Bengali women's value in society at the time depended on their eligibility in the marriage market. Marriage was the primary goal of any woman's life. "Lone women"—whether single, widowed, or (heaven forbid) divorced—were subject to every form of disrespect. Their status was seen as a rebellion.

In the area of beauty, I was a source of ongoing disappointment. I had no interest in spending hours applying Ayurvedic skin and hair care. I had little interest in clothing—except, that is, for shoes.

My passion for shoes began at an early age. One day, I went on an outing with Ma and in a store window, I spied a pair of red Mary Janes, with which I fell promptly and madly in love. To me, these shoes embodied everything that could possibly be right in a world that was often wrong. They were the stuff, I convinced myself, that fairytales were made of. They were red. They were shiny. And they were like nothing I had ever seen. Whoever had red shoes, I honestly believed, would possess magic powers.

Ma saw me pining for them, standing before the store window and trying to touch the shoes through the glass. Later she heard me talking to my sisters about the magic of those ruby slippers.

How my mother managed to come up with the funds to buy them, I do not know. But she did. Maybe she made the purchase because she understood how much they meant to me. Maybe she did it because she was a lover of beauty and could understand the desire to look pretty. Whatever the reason, she bought me those red shoes. They were the most precious gift I had ever received, and I valued them with my life.

***

Days later, I was tucked into bed as usual, dressed in little bloomers and covered by a mosquito net, my red shoes safely under the bed. It had been a hot, uneventful evening. Midway through the night, however, I was awakened by ear-piercing sirens and loud booming noises. The explosions created blinding light in the otherwise dark sky.

It was March 25, 1971, the night the Bangladesh Liberation War began.

For years, Bangladesh had been known as East Pakistan, while modern-day Pakistan was known as West Pakistan. When the Indian subcontinent achieved independence from British rule in 1947, East and West Pakistan were split apart from India and combined in a single majority-Muslim country. Apparently, in the minds of some politicians, this strange arrangement made sense as East and West Pakistan were primarily Muslim, while India had a Hindu majority.

Yet although religion linked East and West Pakistan, there were distinct cultural differences, not to mention the fact that another country—India—ran down the middle. Residents of West Pakistan spoke Urdu and wanted to make the entire country, East and West, Urdu-speaking, while those of us in East Pakistan spoke Bengali and remained extremely proud of our linguistic heritage. There were other differences: West Pakistan was more religiously conservative and less tolerant of the different religions and cultures that mingled in the East, notably the Hindu, Buddhist, Christian, and indigenous minorities. East Pakistan increasingly pushed for greater autonomy within Pakistan, which eventually resulted in West Pakistan attacking its own citizens. Despite West Pakistan's control of the army, the East Pakistanis would prevail, and Bangladesh would be born.

That night, as our war for independence began, I was terrified. I didn't know what was happening, but I knew that I needed to escape. So in the darkness, still dressed only in bloomers, I reached for those magical red shoes. Holding them close to my chest, I ran as fast as I could from the house. I didn't know where I was going, but I knew that I and my red shoes had to get away. It was as if those shoes were the key to my very survival. I hadn't taken the time to put them on my feet, but they were a weapon to help me ward off the terror of that terrible night.

My mother saw me running across the veranda into the garden, which opened up to the street. Picking me up, she carried me, crying and shaking, back into our house, still clutching my red shoes.

A blanket of darkness was falling over our country. With the start of the war with Pakistan, we were entering into a bleak and terrifying time.

Bangladesh's war for independence was even uglier than most wars. There were falling bombs and low-flying aircraft. But there was also genocide. Three million Bengalis were killed over nine months, most of them civilians. West Pakistan sought to impose its rule by wiping out the culture, the intelligentsia, academia—anything and anyone who could define the socioeconomic structure of a new country. Many of those targeted and killed were the intellectual young men of East Pakistan. Every day I heard grownups in our house whisper about someone else from their circle of friends who had been taken away and shot.

But women were targeted as well, taken away by Pakistani soldiers to rape camps. Women in war zones are frequently victims of sexual violence. "Sexual violence is deployed as a weapon of war because to the user, it is cheap, easy and extremely effective in achieving the target of breaking the enemy," writes lawyer Kirthi Jayakumar. "When combatants rape by the dozen, it isn't just about sexual urges, but about seeing the women of the enemy—sometimes just women—breaking before them, physically, emotionally and mentally." The UN now considers sexual violence a weapon of war, not just a consequence of it.

Though I was young, I knew something was very wrong when the women in my home huddled together and spoke of the women they knew who had disappeared. Many were pregnant when they were returned, and the babies were sources of tremendous shame— evidence of the heinous crimes committed against these young women and girls. The rape camps were the crime that had no name. They were a tragedy whose ripple effects would be felt for decades. There has still been no closure or justice.

***

Papa was away from Dhaka during the war. Shortly before the war began, he had left the government in protest of the blatant prejudice by the West Pakistan government against Bengalis and had taken a job in Chittagong, a port city in the southern part of the country. During most of the war, given that Papa was assisting the resistance movement, we didn't know where he was or whether he was alive.

Ma became a source of stability in our home and in the community. Throughout the war, to help others escape the threat of death or rape, Ma hid many cousins, aunts, and friends in our home. At any given time, we had more than twenty people living with us, many of them young women.

When soldiers came around, Ma hid any young men and women living with us at the time out of sight: lying under a bed or crouched in a kitchen storage closet, in the chicken coop, or even on the roof of the house. I watched Ma using all her creativity to protect our relatives. Because I was too young to be taken to any camp or killed, I was allowed to play freely in the house when the Pakistani soldiers came. But I'd been trained. When stern-faced men bent down to ask if anyone else was living in the house with us, I knew to shake my head. I knew to solemnly tell them, "No, sir, we are living here all alone."

Ma's talent for flawlessly speaking multiple languages saved our lives during the war. "We are delighted to welcome you to our house," she would say in Urdu to the soldiers, smiling, as they marched into our house with dirty boots, machine guns, and fatigues. Ma would offer them tea and assure them in her polished Urdu that she would let them know if she saw any freedom fighters snooping around.

It was all an act in front of the soldiers, and we each knew our role well. I would stand and watch in silence, eyes wide open and palms sweating. Those guns were so frightening, and the soldiers were so big. The moment they left, Ma would hug me and whisper in my ear, "Once again, you were so brave." If I was brave, it was because I was watching her. There she was, courageously chatting with soldiers, while relatives and friends cowered in closets and under beds.

It's often said that men make war and women live with the consequences. That's the truth—in part. But the brave women of Bangladesh and many other countries across the globe demonstrate that while women suffer the consequences of war, they don't always see themselves as victims. They heroically carry on. They come up with solutions—they *become* the solutions—that lead toward nation-building and sustainable peace.

CHAPTER THREE

The Meaning of Independence

I've witnessed two plane crashes in my life. The first was in 1971, during the war. At the time, a plane falling out of the sky and landing not far from the house did not strike me as odd. When your childhood is full of fireballs and loud booms and smoke, otherwise extraordinary events become the norm.

Things had been falling from the sky for some time. The nightly bombs started the first night of the war, when I had run out of the house clutching my red shoes. Bombers flying low over our home were a constant reminder of war. By day, sirens filled the air, often drowning out the rat-a-tat-tat of gunfire.

On the day of the crash, I was playing on the veranda with my third sister Tazneen. We had been playing snakes and ladders when we heard the roar of engines. The noise was close: closer than normal, deafeningly close. So, naturally, we all climbed the stairs to the roof to get a better look.

That's when we saw the source of the sound: two aircraft. One was an American-made fighter, flown by the Pakistani air force. The other was a Russian-made fighter, flown by the Indian air force. At this point, India had joined the war to assist East Pakistan to gain independence.

The air was cool. I wore a thin sweater, a hand-me-down from my elder sisters that I pulled close as we huddled on the roof to watch. We sat transfixed, mouths agape and eyes wide, as the planes chased one another in an aerial version of cat and mouse. For me, watching the planes whiz by seemed like a private air show, and I had a front-row seat.

And so when the dogfight came to a screeching and deafening halt and the Pakistani plane went crashing to the ground a few football fields away from our backyard, I wasn't traumatized. I was excited! Something big—*really* big—had happened, and I had seen the whole thing.

Thirty years later and a world away, my adult self would witness a second crash. That time, there would be no feeling of excitement, only dread.

***

A few weeks after the plane crash behind our house, the war was over: East Pakistan had defeated West Pakistan, and Bangladesh was born. Despite the destruction everywhere, pride and celebration electrified the air. "Joy Bangla! Joy Bangla!" I remember shouting at the top of my voice, "Victory to Bengal!," when we heard the news of victory and we all rushed out into the street, jumping and screaming for joy.

Our joy increased with the news that Papa was coming home. Ma burst into tears and smiles when she received a long-awaited call from him after phone lines were restored. We found out later that Papa had used the house he was living in, in the hilly part of Chittagong, to hide and assist the freedom fighters. For Papa, this war was long overdue. He had marched as a student in the language movement in 1952 to protest West Pakistan's mandate to supplant Bengali, our mother tongue, with Urdu as the national language. He had been shot at and injured, but many of his friends had not been that lucky. They had given their lives for our language. This war of independence was his moment to even the score for his fallen friends.

Although the war had ended, the tragedies continued, etched on the faces and bodies of the millions now trying to piece together their lives and build a country from nothing with their bare hands. People with starvation written on their faces were everywhere. Emerging from the war, the new country of Bangladesh needed to be built from scratch, and everyone had their own idea of how to do it. Western countries poured in economic aid with strings attached, while multilateral organizations, international nonprofits, and multilateral banks dictated the terms of engagement of their liking.

The Western colonial mindset was still very much at work. It was as though the former colonizers, and the institutions they created, thought they knew best how to rebuild a country they had helped destroy in the first place. Many of them had assisted West Pakistan, a key Western ally in the Cold War, with military aid during the war. But now, they assumed they should be the ones shaping the new country. And the people of the country themselves, what did they want? No one asked us.

For years following the independence, our young country suffered through political power struggles, driven by personality and military politics. While some children have school canceled for snow days, we became accustomed to "military coup days." Every few months, we'd wake up to the sounds of gunfire, tanks, or bombs. Another coup, or some other political change, meant there would be no school that day.

How do you piece together the building blocks of a country? How do you create a functioning economy, rebuild infrastructure, and include everyone in the peacebuilding effort? In trying to answer these questions, Bangladesh struggled with socialist idealism and capitalist pressure. As a country, it benefited from economic aid but also suffered humiliation from wealthy individuals, organizations, and governments that only saw our hunger and poverty, and thought they had a right to shape us in return for aid. Bangladesh was a pawn in the Cold War game. We had neither significant natural resources nor a strategic position, and we lacked the power to make our voices heard.

***

As I learned about what had happened to my country, I became determined to be nobody's pawn. In reality, though, I had little control over my life. Adults around me constantly admonished me that everything—our personal lives, our country's predicament—was due to fate. Fate was our duty to accept.

Life was filled with lessons in how to be a good Muslim girl and how to make the most of the little we had. Every weekend the mullah, a junior Muslim clergyperson from the local mosque, would visit our home to make sure my sisters and I were memorizing the Quran, performing the prescribed rituals, and following the Islamic rules for girls. So after finishing the day's chores, we four sisters would sit in a row on worn-out prayer mats on the floor, our heads and bodies covered. After doing the proper *wudu* (the ablution, or ritual purification, of the body before prayers), and with the Quran opened in front of us, we would read the Arabic scripture and repeat the prayers after the mullah. Then we would listen to his sermon.

"Remember what the Quran says," he would say. "The Quran clearly states your role in society. You are girls. Girls are weak. You need to be taken care of by a man. Remember: your position in society is to serve your elders and the men. When you get married, you need to listen to your husband." The sermon would end with the usual caution that any deviation from the rules would put us on the road to hell and place a curse on the family.

Sometimes I would push back: "Show me where the Quran says that I need to listen to a man," I'd say. But the mullah did not tolerate my insolence, and his complaints would lead to scolding from Ma.

"Why can't you ever accept anything that is told to you?" she'd ask me. "Why do you make everything such a fight? Who are you to question the Quran? This is fate. Accept fate."

***

Each Friday, the holy day for Muslims, we gave alms to the poor. My siblings and I would wait at the gate of our house to give a cup of uncooked rice to the poor, sharing the rice we got from our government ration. I would collect the clay pot of uncooked rice and a scoop made of half a coconut shell and take up my position by the gate. There I would dispense cups of rice to the line of beggars at our door.

"Make sure you only give one cup of rice to each beggar," Bubu would say to me with a smile. "We need to make the rice last for others; we don't want to leave anyone disappointed."

This was our ritual every Friday. Giving out rice left me with mixed feelings. On one hand, I liked sharing with others the little we had, ensuring them a meal for the day. On the other, the act left me feeling frustrated. A cupful of rice each week? That did not really change the lives of the poor. They kept coming back every week. I was not solving anything for them. The handouts served as a stopgap and did not create any long-lasting solution.

When I questioned our ritual, Bubu, who was a very pious woman, would tell me how many *sawab* (blessings) I was getting from the poor because of the rice we donated. The blessings in turn would make good things happen to me—like getting a rich husband. That logic left me even more troubled. If the poor kept on returning for a cup of rice, I would eventually get a good husband? The transaction seemed unfair. By that logic, if the poor girl at our door wanted a rich husband, should she give *me* a cup of rice? None of it made any sense.

In the same way, it troubled me when Papa would come home from his new government job complaining about yet another meeting with a donor—usually a rich country or multilateral bank lending money to Bangladesh. "They have their own idea of what is good for our country," Papa would say ruefully.

Bangladesh was not all that different from the beggar who received my rice without being empowered to purchase their own. I was part of a system putting a tiny Band-Aid on a massive, festering wound, and the rich countries were too. How can we heal a wound if we don't question the healing method? How can we just accept what *is* and assume it's the way it should be?

Maybe it's not the poor people—or the poor country—who are at fault, I started to think. Maybe we should evaluate the system that keeps them there.

CHAPTER FOUR

Should and Should Not

After the war was over, money remained tight. Ma had to make Papa's meager government salary serve a large immediate family as well as his extended family. Even with Dadu's government pension and rent from the tenant upstairs, we had to count every *paisa*. Each of us sisters had just two or three dresses or *shalwar kameez*, a long tunic dress worn with harem pants and a long scarf.

Ma's and Bubu's old saris became clothes and blankets, and Ma also made all our sweaters. At the bazaar, she would buy donated sweaters that came in shiploads from rich countries. She would wash and rewash the sweaters, undo the knitting, and make balls of yarn. Many evenings our crowded living room would be strewn with piles of yarn that we all would help Ma sort. She would pore over intricate patterns and knit gorgeous sweaters, ponchos, and hats—everything we needed for those three months of Dhaka winter. Thanks to Ma, my siblings and I always had the most fashionable sweaters and cardigans.

Ma was also an excellent baker, and in those days, when there were very few baked goods in the stores, she carved out a niche for herself in our community. She made bread, rolls, cakes, and cupcakes to supply to stores and to sell at the community fair, and she made decent money from it. Nobody knew that this woman, with such a sophisticated exterior, was stitching and knitting our clothes at night and running a small business on the side. Women did not run busi-nesses, so Ma's work was not really a "business" in our eyes. It was simply what she did so that the gentle poverty in which our family languished would not be visible to society. There was simply no end to the creative ways that Ma could make ends meet.

My sisters would help Ma with her baking. I was often banished from the tiny kitchen, as I not only had no knack for baking but also refused to follow a recipe. For me, a recipe was a suggestion, and my precise mother was not having any of that.

My job was to collect the eggs from the chicken coop. Ma had set up an elaborate chicken coop with fifty chickens, which supplied eggs for her baking and extra income by selling the rest. These chickens were her pride and joy. They got special feed, and cabbage was hung from the ceiling of the coop for them to peck at through-out the day. These fifty chickens and the two roosters brought in a substantial income for Ma, and she was not about to cut corners with their care.

Every day I cleaned the coop, fed the chickens, and collected eggs. I did not know which job was the worst, but collecting eggs was cer-tainly the most stressful. The chickens would never lay the eggs in the same place, which meant I had to look around for them, giving the roosters time to prepare a defense. I was taking away their potential babies, and they would defend their own by orchestrating elaborate attacks. They would strut around and then break into runs before aiming flying kicks at my legs, which they cut with their hind spur. It was terrifying, but my complaints about the attacks fell on deaf ears. Ma would not listen. "You are just being dramatic, as always. How can you be afraid of these roosters?' she would say.

Then one day my salvation came. I was sick, so Ma had to collect the eggs herself. Lo and behold, one of the roosters attacked her. That night we ate rooster for dinner. There was no discussion of the attack at the dinner table, but my sisters and I had a hard time not laughing aloud.

***

Given our financial constraints, as children, we had no concept of pocket money. Even requesting a few *taka*, equivalent to a couple of pennies at that time, for a piece of candy was asking for luxury. I decided that I needed to figure out how to make some money. Around this time, I was maintaining several thriving pen pal friendships with girls around the world, including one in Germany and one in the Netherlands. The nuns in the Catholic school I attended encouraged us to have these friendships so we could practice our English. Although I had no frame of reference for what they wrote about—beaches, dances, fashion, boy issues—I loved receiving their letters, each of which bore a wonderful foreign stamp.

I loved those stamps, and I spent hours studying them. I would look up the countries in our leather-bound encyclopedia set, my father's most prized possession. Those volumes were my window to the world of history, geography, and politics.

The more I glimpsed the world through my stamps, the more stamps I wanted. I begged my father to buy me a special stamp book during one of his overseas trips. I also asked my pen pals to send me any stamps they could get their hands on. I started asking relatives for stamps, and soon I turned every conversation into an opportunity to source stamps. In a few years' time, I had an extensive collection, including some rarities.

Eventually I had enough duplicates to encourage my friends to start stamp collections. This was my first taste of "seeding" enterprises. I would give a few stamps to my friends, and they would start their own collections. Then, when they had built up their collections, I would have them give me back a few more stamps than what I originally gave them. When enough of my friends had collections, I started trading, exchanging more valuable stamps for bundles of less valuable stamps. From barter, I progressed to selling. Soon I had a full-fledged business with several revenue streams. Now that I had income, I could buy pickles and ice cream from the carts outside of school, all without ever telling Ma.

My business was going very well until I got my first taste of the perils of accounts receivable. In order to expand my market, I had sold some stamps to the neighborhood boys. Initially, they didn't resist paying me, but one day they said, "Girls shouldn't even collect stamps. You are *selling* them, so we won't pay you." I had no leverage, because I knew I was not supposed to be earning money, and I could not go to any adult for help.

When I refused to back down, the boys complained to their mothers. Before I knew it, my own mother's wrath had descended. Ma gave me a severe beating because I had brought shame to her and the family, and she took away my stamp collection. I begged and pleaded with her to give it back, and I promised not to trade or sell stamps anymore. But Ma did not budge. Dadu took my mother's side. Papa was absent. And Bubu just shook her head. "This is what happens when you don't accept your position in life," she said.

Years later, I asked my mother what had happened to my collection. Her words were a precursor to the lessons I would eventually learn about being a woman entrepreneur in a man's world. "Oh, those silly stamps?" she responded offhandedly. "I gave them to one of your male cousins years ago. You know girls aren't supposed to collect stamps."

***

Still flat-chested and climbing trees, I became a woman on my twelfth birthday. From my three older sisters, I knew that a girl "becomes a woman" when she gets her period. Ma had warned me about what was coming. "It is a horrible thing, but this is a process every girl has to go through," she told me. "You become a woman, and your life changes forever."

April is the hottest time of the year throughout South Asia. The earth is scorched and cracked, and if you pour water on the ground, you can see steam rise. I did not let any of that get to me, though, because April meant it was my birthday. It was my day: the one day I didn't have to share or receive as a hand-me-down.

My brother, Isa, was born five years after I was, after the war. Having finally produced a son, Ma had now fulfilled her duties in the eyes of her parents, her husband, and his family; and she had earned the respect she craved. Isa's birth was like the coming of the messiah, and there was joy and celebration galore. Isa represented joy to my family both because he was a boy and because the timing of his birth became the symbol of hope after the war.

Thus, even with our humble means, our family celebrated Isa's birthday every year with balloons, a cake, gifts, and friends. We girls never had birthday parties and were told that we should be happy because our brother's party was *our* party, too. As the boy and the baby in the family, he brought happiness to our lives: that was the narrative, and we had to accept it.

This year, a party was finally within my reach. Much to Papa's chagrin, Ma had taken a loan from the bank to buy a small piece of land and put up a tiny two-bedroom rental house on it. The house was now rented out, and we had extra income. We suddenly had a little more of everything. Meals changed from potato curry with a few pieces of chicken thrown in to chicken curry with potatoes on the side. With the occasional and precious cup of milk we could now have a spoonful of chocolate malt Ovaltine.

Most years, the only gift we girls would receive on our birthdays was a set of clothes: a dress until we were about twelve and then a shalwar kameez. Our birthday outfits were made from old saris of Ma's or Bubu's—but not this year. "You can choose the material and pattern for your dress this year to wear at your party," Ma had announced a few weeks before my birthday. I could not believe my good fortune! But Ma kept her word, and off we went to the market together to buy the material for a dress.

In the fabric store were reels of beautifully patterned cloths. There were rows and rows of rolled-up material behind the shop workers, who were all men. Today the men were animated, and I enjoyed watching and listening to Ma talk fashion with them in their village dialects. They had no more idea of fashion than I did, but that did not stop them from having opinions: "No, this is too transparent. It will give ideas to boys." "Yes, this color is high fashion now." Men in our society all had strong opinions on what women should wear.

After selecting a soft blue cotton-linen blend, we stopped next at the neighborhood tailor, Mr. Ahmed. He was an elderly man, a migrant from the Indian province of Uttar Pradesh, who had brought along with him beautiful needlework skills. His shop was in a neighbor's garage. The shop had no sign or name, but everyone in the neighborhood knew where it was.

Mr. Ahmed could only speak Urdu. He loved Ma because not only would she speak to him in Urdu but she would also bring him fruits from our house each time she came to his shop. They chatted about life and embroidery patterns, and Ma inquired about his business.

Ma's interest in Mr. Ahmed's business, contrasted by her disapproval of my stamp trading, puzzled me. They talked for a long time. Years later I would find out that Ma frequently advised small business owners like Mr. Ahmed. She was helping them get started, sending customers their way, and assisting them with business development. Once her children had grown up, she gave money to these microbusinesses to help them grow, all without expecting any financial return. Her only requirement of the shop owners and entrepreneurs she assisted was that they agree to educate their daughters.

Every year at the Bengali New Year on April 15, there would be a line of shop owners—the tailor, the silver jeweler, the sari shopkeeper, the sweet store owner—at our door to get their new financial logbook signed by Ma. She was their Lakshmi, the Hindu goddess of good fortune, and their good luck charm. As the Bengali tradition goes, a business needs to have the touch of a Lakshmi to start their fiscal year, and Ma provided that touch for many. Years later, with my own business, I would often crave a Lakshmi who would bless my business with her good luck and set it on the right course.

As a woman maneuvering a restrictive society, Ma contained many dualities. I think that making small changes happen in the community, in her own way, gave her the power she craved but could not openly wield. She could help women in society by exerting soft power on these small businesses.

In public, of course, Ma never openly questioned her society and religion, which did not grant women power, freedom, or choice. But she went about her business of quietly advising entrepreneurs—and requiring that they send their daughters to school.

***

Even though our oven was old, with a broken door propped up with a stick, Ma baked delicious cakes. This oven produced hundreds of loaves of breads, buns, and various forms of fruitcakes, all in high demand through Ma's hidden marketplace.

Tazneen, in her quiet way, was Ma's helpful hand. Measuring the flour, butter, and sugar and chopping the preserved fruits: Tazneen was always one step ahead of Ma and soon became her baking assistant.

"I am very happy that you're having a birthday party," Tazneen whispered to me in the kitchen as she prepared ingredients. "I never had the courage to ask for one, but I am glad you did. I will make sure that you have a fabulous cake."

I felt selfish and guilty when Tazneen said this to me. She, too, had never had a party. But unlike me, she had accepted her fate. That was the case with all the women in my life: they simply accepted their fate. Would my life be easier if I accepted mine? I knew the answer was yes, but I was unwilling to accept this answer. That is why I wore Ma down with my negotiation to allow for me to have a birthday party just like Isa had every year.

"We have to do the icing quickly or else it will melt in the heat," Ma instructed. "You need to work swiftly and not make a mess . . . or irritate me." I promised Ma I would be a good girl. But as we started mixing the butter, icing sugar, and chocolate powder, my mouth started drooling. Each time Ma looked away, I dipped my finger and took a lick, then quickly wiped my fingers on my dress. I kept tasting the icing the entire time we were working on the cake.

It was a gorgeous chocolate cake with pretty flower designs. Tazneen and Ma had done their magic. But even before we finished the final touches, my stomach started aching. I must have eaten too much of the icing, I thought. I did not tell Ma, because then she would figure out that I had been sneaking the icing. My stomach pain got worse and, when I went to the bathroom, I saw that some of the chocolate icing had, by some mysterious means, gotten on my underwear. How had it gotten from my dress to my panties?

Then, in a flash, I understood. This was something more serious. Something having to do with womanhood and fate, with growing up and accepting one's lot, wrapped up in shame and responsibility.

***

Dadu was sitting in his worn-out chair in the crowded living room. Dadu sat in that chair for hours: watching TV, giving legal advice to the countless people who still came to him seeking it, or helping us with our homework.

I dreaded going over to him. He was the ultimate authority in our house, and even more so when he was sitting in that chair. His demeanor was always very formal and British, as though he had never left his position as a judge under the British Raj. He was still the judge in our house. My grandmother, mother, and sisters—all the women would come to him for his wisdom and judgment.

I had finally worked up my nerve to tell my mother about the onset of my period, and she was taking me to talk to my grandfather in the living room. "Dadu, a man, is going to tell me how I have become a woman?" I asked in disbelief.

Ma looked at me with sad resolve. "Your birthday is always a tough day for me. You came to me as a girl, the fourth one. Now, twelve years later, Allah wanted to remind me again that you are a girl and made you have your period on your birthday. Such is my fate and yours. Now, once I show you how to manage this, you must go to Dadu, who will tell you what it means to be a woman."

My chest hurt from guilt. I had let my parents down: once by being born a girl and now again by becoming a woman on my birthday. So here I was, gingerly walking over to the throne of authority to hear from my grandfather about my destiny as a woman. I pulled over a stool and took a seat by Dadu's feet, showing proper deference.

Surprisingly, Dadu's stern face softened, and he stroked my head. He solemnly took my hand and said, "When your mother was pregnant with you, we were all excited that, at last, we were going to have a boy. Our daughter was finally going to receive the respect she deserved from our society. But Allah had other plans, and you were born." He told me once again about chura moni: the auspicious moment of my birth, the sad fact that I had been born a girl.

Now, on my birthday, Dadu continued: "Now you are a woman. Congratulations! You can now serve your purpose in your life: to have babies. Now that your body is ready to have babies, you must never be alone with boys or men in a room. If you are ever alone with a boy and he touches you, you will get a baby in your tummy. A baby in your tummy before marriage is a fate worse than death. So no more playing with the neighborhood boys. You also now need to cover your legs and arms and wear shalwar kameez with a scarf all the time. No more biking in the streets for hours, and no more climbing trees."

With each sentence he said, I could feel a strong net cinching a bit more tightly around me. I did not want to become a woman. Tears started rolling down my cheeks.

"Your Bubu will let you know about all the rituals that go with being a woman," he said. "This one week you are considered dirty, so you can't say prayers or touch the Quran or even touch certain foods, as they will spoil if you touch them. Once the week is over, you have to remove all the unnecessary hair from your body except for your head and take a special bath before you can be clean again to join the world."

I left the foot of my grandfather's chair and went to get dressed for the party, which was now suspended in time between girlhood and womanhood. I put on my new blue dress, and I put a matching clip in my hair. With a heavy heart, I got ready for the first and last birthday party in my life. In that one afternoon, I learned that I was a woman, that society controlled my body, and that I was untouchable for one week each month. I may have been born at the auspicious moment of chura moni, but no great heights were preordained for me.

I did not tell my friends what had happened. We played tag. I dashed around Ma's rose bushes, I squealed, I laughed, and I got my beautiful blue dress dirty. But I did not care. It was my last chance to be myself. The moment my friends left, my childhood would end and womanhood would begin.

CHAPTER FIVE

Defying the Status Quo

Being a good Bangladeshi woman is difficult when you are awkward and gawky. "How come you have not blossomed yet?" my aunts and the neighborhood aunties would say when they saw me. "At this rate, you will never find a husband."

"Good thing I won't need a husband to take care of me!" I fired back. "I can take care of myself!" Those retorts always earned a scolding from my mother. The messages were manifold. You need to learn to sew. You need to learn to cook. You need to know how to arrange flowers. You need to know how to sing. You must know all the Bengali and Muslim rituals, because you will need to carry them out with your family.

I had watched my elder sisters all dutifully embrace this curriculum of womanhood. But I could not. The rules, the expectations, the restrictions: all of it was suffocating. I knew I needed to escape from this, but how?

As if answering my prayers, one fateful afternoon, Ma simply said, "We need to talk. We will have a family meeting tonight."

Family meetings were always stressful. Our parents would summon all of us to their bedroom and usually share bad news, typically concerning finances. Or it might concern a potential marriage proposal for Mahreen that would require us to be on our best behavior when the suitor's family came to check her out.

When we had gathered, Papa announced, "We are moving to the Philippines." We were all stunned, but he continued, "I have been selected to represent South Asia on the board of the Asian Development Bank. It will come with a good salary, so at last, we can save for your weddings and for Isa's education overseas."

My head was spinning. I knew the Philippines from my geography class and stamp collection: 7,500 islands, many of them volcanic. Under Spanish rule for four hundred years before the United States took over in the 1898 Spanish-American War. Then a US colony until World War II. Most importantly, the Philippines was a very Americanized society. From all that I had seen on television and read in magazines I believed America meant freedom.

Although my father never said these words, I had received a welcome message behind his news: This is how you start to escape. This is how you begin to leave.

***

Manila is a bustling city like Dhaka, but in the early 1980s, it was much more modern. There were shopping malls with movie theaters where we could get popcorn and soda. The television was in color and had multiple channels, and everyone wore blue jeans. And it seemed like everyone could speak American English: rolling their *r*s, elongating their *a*s, and using just the right nasal touch.

My poor English, however, was soon holding me back at my new school, the International School of Manila. And I could not share my struggles in school with anyone at home out of fear that my parents would follow through with their threat to send me back to Bangladesh. So I came up with some creative learning tools. I became a devotee of *Reader's Digest*'s "Enrich Your Word Power" section, and I set out to learn ten English words every day.

"Can I have your old *Reader's Digests*?" became my refrain. Teachers, the librarian, and parents of new friends all gave me their old copies. When my 6:00 a.m. alarm rang, I would spring out of bed and, even before brushing my teeth, I would pore over the ten new words I had written the night before. Just as I memorized prayers from the Quran when I was young—eyes shut tight and rapidly repeating them in my head with my lips moving in unison—so I memorized these new English words. Brushing my teeth, I would repeat them; eating breakfast, I would repeat them; walking to school, I would keep repeating them.

As the year rolled on and I started becoming more comfortable with English, the material at school started getting easier for me. As soon as I got the hang of the English terms, I skipped to the higher classes. Once again, I had to catch up, but I was relieved to regain confidence in my academic abilities.

It was in the Philippines that I discovered the discipline of economics. Until high school, I knew little about world history besides what I had learned through my stamp collection and my individual studies. In my early teenage years, I had become fascinated with the subject of genocide and tried to understand how such evil could happen—be it the 1971 war in Bangladesh or the atrocities of World War II. So much suffering, so many human lives lost! What struck me then was how often wars are economically motivated. As I learned more about economics, dotted lines began connecting in my head. I began to see how the desire to accumulate money and resources lies at the heart of many political and social struggles.

From the fifteenth century onward, Europe enriched itself by creating trade routes and forming colonies all over the world. The riches of Bengal and the rest of India were siphoned off to make the United Kingdom a rich nation. I would pore over my history and economic books for hours, trying to understand how companies could take over entire nations—be it the British East India Company in India or the Dutch East India Company in Indonesia or, in more modern times, companies like Del Monte in the Philippines. Commerce could determine a nation's future. Trade in spices, silk, fruit, or even opium lay behind the rise and fall of empires.

I became particularly intrigued by the link between politics and economics. When my economics teacher Mr. Ralph would lecture about monetary policies, I kept asking him questions. Why did the government select this monetary policy? Why not mix it with the right fiscal policy? What political calculus was motivating them? Mr. Ralph would get irritated. "You don't have to solve the world's problems now," he told me. "Just focus on the theories that you will need to pass the test."

But I wanted to know how theories applied in the real world. If the Marshall Plan could get Europe and Japan off the ground after World War II, why didn't Bangladesh have such an economic recovery plan? Where were the reparations for Bangladesh from the Pakistani government—or, for that matter, from the US government, which had backed Pakistan in the war? Who determined what was considered a First, Second, and Third World country? Why was economic aid to some countries still politically motivated when, over hundreds of years, the West had taken trillions of dollars of wealth out of these countries to develop their own economies?

I would eventually realize that economic systems could create the oppressors and the oppressed. Could they also give prosperity to all? I knew I needed to find out how to create and wield this kind of power. I just had no idea how.

***

One of the starkest differences between Dhaka and Manila in the early 1980s was the sheer number of women walking on the streets and engaging in commerce in Manila. By contrast, Dhaka seemed like a city of men. There, the buses were filled with men. The broken, garbage-strewn sidewalks were filled with men. And the cars were driven by men. The few women in the bus or on the road took care to dress especially modestly, with their heads covered, so that they did not catch anyone's attention.

That is why, on my bike rides in Dhaka, I had always dressed as a boy, wearing Papa's old pants, a loose shirt, and a cap tucking in my hair. As a girl visible on the street, I would have been in danger. Women were supposed to be invisible. Despite their invisible status, women in Bangladesh, similar to other developing countries, carried the burden of work in the agriculture sector, which was the economic lifeblood of the country. Decades later, women laborers would become the foundation of the thriving Bangladeshi garment industry. Women learned to be both invisible and industrious.

That was not the case in the Philippines. Women walked in the street on their way to work. Women worked in offices, schools, universities, stores, and restaurants. The economy seemed to rest on the shoulders of women.

Despite women's progress, however, the Philippines was still a divided nation of haves and have-nots. A handful of rich families, aided by a corrupt government, controlled the wealth and economy of the nation. President Ferdinand Marcos and his wife, Imelda, were at the center of this. Their excessive and corrupt lifestyle started becoming more than a rumor.

"Did you know that in the Malacanayang Palace they have trees made of emeralds, because Imelda is allergic to plants?" someone at school would say. "Apparently they have billions of dollars stashed away outside of the country," someone else would whisper. These conversations became louder and more frequent among Filipino friends of mine who were on scholarships at the school.

And then there were the rich Filipino kids, who looked and acted completely European and American. Many of them had more European than Filipino ancestry, continuing the colonial legacy of interconnection between race and wealth. There were often tense moments between these two groups, and students in my school increasingly separated into factions. What started as heated arguments escalated into physical fights. What one faction saw as social justice the other saw as an attack on their lifestyles. Eventually the school administration stepped in. No more political discussions among students would be permitted, administrators said. This was effective in maintaining order at school, but it did nothing to change the direction the country was heading.

The tension inside the school was a microcosm of what was happening in the streets. The opposition party—which espoused progressive ideals, demanded an end to corruption, and was led by Benigno

Aquino Jr. from exile in the United States—was getting stronger and more vocal. There were frequent peaceful demonstrations in the streets as university students and others marched to protest extreme inequality. In this tense situation, Aquino announced that he was going to return to the Philippines.

For me, watching the slow start of the democratic movement was exciting. We had witnessed endless political turmoil in Bangladesh, and it was exhilarating to watch another society striving for the goal of social equity and beginning to develop a political voice with a very different approach.

***

"Come quickly! It's starting!" shouted Isa from the TV room. I ran upstairs to find my whole family glued to the television. Benigno Aquino was coming back from self-exile in the United States to lead a revolution. The thousands who had gathered at the airport to receive him went wild when his plane landed. Aquino was the symbol of hope and change for a country that was hungry for both. Rumors had been flying at school and all over the city about what would happen to Aquino if he returned. Everyone expected that Marcos would imprison him again, but how would it play out? There was speculation around his safety, and he was rumored to be wearing a bulletproof vest.

The plane door opened, and Aquino emerged with a big smile. He waved at the cheering spectators. Then, as he came down the steps from the plane, one of the guards took out a gun and shot him in the head. The opposition leader had been shot, live, on television.

At that moment, we knew the Philippines faced an enormous change. Chaos, confusion, violence, uncertainty about who was in power and how they would work with opposing perspectives: it all seemed like a page out of the political drama of Bangladesh. Ma would later joke that we must have brought the political turmoil of Bangladesh with us to the Philippines.

Coming from Bangladesh, we were veterans of political and student unrest, but we had not witnessed civil disobedience on this scale. There was a sense of innocence and optimism in the students marching and chanting while tucking flowers in the soldiers' rifles. It seemed to be an effective movement that heralded a much-needed revolution.

But not everyone welcomed this People Power revolution. As unrest escalated, so did the pressure on the privileged class, who benefited from the Marcos regime, to forego some of their power. Any type of social or economic reform would mean the privileged class would have the most to lose. Just a handful of families in the Philippines owned 90 percent of the land, its vast resources, the private sector, the banking system, and everything else that went hand in hand with economic and political power. Since many of my classmates belonged to this group, the school started receiving bomb threats.

Throughout history and across the globe, economic inequality is supported by social structures that benefit the powerful and bolster the status quo. Most of the time, these structures go unchallenged, often because change seems impossible. But when things reach a breaking point, sometimes sparks of defiant optimism create a moment when even the most difficult change seems possible. Bangladesh had witnessed such a moment in 1971. This was such a time in the Philippines.

This energy was in the air in Manila as I approached the end of my high school years. While this struggle was not my own, I empathized with the passion of the Filipino people. What the Philippines would make of this moment was not yet clear, but it seemed like a new beginning with endless possibilities.

Where my own path would lead was also not yet clear. But I felt myself standing on a precipice, ready to take flight.

PART II

Search for the Source of Power

CHAPTER SIX

Rebel with a Cause

Sitting in the window seat, in the second to last row on the flight to New York via Tokyo, put me right between the smoking section and the toilets. Buying a cheap ticket last minute meant taking whatever was available—in this case, a seat in which I had to breathe in smoke and foul odors for the more-than-thirty-hour journey from Manila.

As an asthmatic prone to motion sickness, the situation was less than ideal, but I didn't care. I smiled and took another puff of my inhaler to keep my asthma at bay. Even shortness of breath could not diminish my excitement for the new life awaiting me.

Outside the window, I saw the mountainous terrain of Alaska. Covered in snow, the jagged mountain peaks looked strangely unreal, like pictures of the surface of the moon. From thirty thousand feet, I was seeing snow for the first time. I had to pinch myself. I was on the longest journey of my life, all alone, with a few dollars and my passport in my bag. It hardly seemed possible that it was all real.

US college admissions fever had struck my class in eleventh grade. Suddenly it became the main topic of conversation. Sitting in the guidance counselor's office, studying university brochures, I saw pictures of happy students—almost all of them white—walking among grand old buildings on carpets of red and yellow leaves. I had heard that leaves change color in the autumn in America. I wanted to be there with those students. I wanted to learn and be a part of a world that celebrated my learning.

"I picked up an application form for Lady Sri Ram College at Delhi University," my father informed me one evening over dinner.

"Oh, but I don't want to go to India for university," I told him.

"Why? What's wrong with India? Some of the top universities in the world are there!" my father said, irritated. "We have always made it clear that we will support you and your sisters' higher education, but it is India, Philippines or Bangladesh. There are no other alternatives."

Isa and Tazneen both left the table. Ma was busy in the kitchen. I looked down at my plate and took a deep breath. Then I looked straight into my father's eyes and said with a steady voice, "I want to go to America for university."

"Well, yes, you can go to America with your husband if he does his higher education there. But for your education, it is Asia."

My three elder sisters had never questioned my parents' decisions. But I was not my sisters. "What husband?" I asked. "Why is my life always planned around an imaginary husband? I want to go to America for my education."

"America is a racist place," my father added, calmly, trying a different tactic. "When I was at Harvard, I visited Tennessee to do research, and the restaurants would not serve my friends and me because I was colored. I couldn't believe that Black people in America had to endure this humiliation! Yes, that was 1961, and things have changed for the better. But why would you want to go to a country that treats its own people as second-class citizens?"

I granted him that point. "Yes, America treats people of color badly. But it is still a country where you can fight back and protest. You can push for social justice. And how about our own country? How badly do we treat women and minorities in Bangladesh? Do you want me to go back to a country where my life will be dictated by my husband and my in-laws? Where I will get respect from society only if I produce a son?"

I got up and left the table. The more my parents said no, the more determined I became to go to America.

The next day, I sat with Bubu at the table, having an afternoon snack and conducting my daily monologue with her. Dadu had died a couple of years ago, and while Bubu had never said much before, after Dadu's death, she barely spoke. I missed her defiant spirit, her smile as she smoked Dadu's hookah, and her gentle powers of persuasion as she spoke to him while cooking up the traditional dishes he loved. It was as if her rebelliousness and creativity were wrapped around Dadu. The man who had controlled her life seemingly took that life with him when he died.

"Bubu, I want to go to America. I want to study there. Can you pray for me? I have big plans for myself. I know I can achieve them if I go to America."

Bubu said nothing and just stared into the distance. I knew she could hear me. I looked at her and thought to myself with sudden clarity: I don't want your life. I don't want to live for a man. I need to leave you and this world behind so that I can come back prepared to change it. Change it so that we as women don't have to justify our existence and lack of voice.

Much to my parent's disapproval, I applied to a handful of American universities, focusing on schools with strong financial aid and women's universities. A few months later, I received a telegram from Smith College with word that I had been accepted. I was so happy that I could barely breathe.

***

So there I was with a single suitcase and a heart full of hope on my way to Smith College. Because I was going to America against my parents' wishes, they were no longer financially responsible for me. Smith had offered me a very good financial aid package, but at seventeen, I would have to work to cover the gap and for personal expenses. I didn't mind. I was still in shock that my parents had allowed me to come to America all by myself.

I peered out of the plane window at the New York City skyline. "Ladies and gentlemen, to your right, you can see the beautiful Lady

Liberty," the captain announced over the loudspeaker. I searched for her in the darkness, and there she was, the Statue of Liberty. Miles away in the air, I could see her: holding her torch, which beckoned us all. She was majestic, glowing, and welcoming. I exhaled and smiled.

At the baggage carousel, I collected my suitcase and entered a sea of people pushing, shoving, and asking if I needed a taxi. I was desperately looking for a familiar face, and at last I saw Kakku (Uncle), my father's younger brother who was working at the UN. Kakku was smiling and came over to give me a hug. A wave of relief washed over me, and I hugged him back. I had always liked Kakku. He was kind, polite, and very much the diplomat he had trained to be.

Kakku drove me to his apartment on Roosevelt Island, a small island in the East River with a cluster of apartment buildings where many UN folks lived. As I was getting ready for bed, my parents called to check that I had arrived safely. I could not say much because I knew I might burst out crying.

After hanging up, I drifted over to the window and wrapped myself tightly in the kantha that Ma had made for me from leftover saris before I had left home. It was her way of forgiving my insolence, and of passing on to me her hope, her protection, and her solace. I looked out at the glittering lights of Manhattan in the distance with tears streaming down my cheeks, feeling so very alone.

***

"You need to hurry up with the tomatoes and then get to the carrots!" the chef barked. Chopping vegetables was one of my many jobs on campus. Life at Smith had started at full force: going to classes, adjusting to an entirely new life and new people, speaking only English, and working every minute possible between the kitchen, dining room, library, and babysitting. There were never enough hours in the day.

Although I was used to housework, working more than thirty hours a week on top of classes and college activities was not easy. This job was fine, but chopping vegetables for eighty people in two hours' time before running back to class was rough.

"No, you can't put back the milk that has been sitting out for an hour. You have to throw it out!" Sophie was exasperated. "Girl, did you live in a cave?"

"Sure, call a culture of over a billion people a cave," I said sarcastically. "No, I am just not used to throwing out food. I expect to reheat the milk and finish it up. But it's OK. When in Rome . . . " I said, pouring the milk down the drain.

Scarcity makes you approach basic necessities with care and attention. At home, we did not throw out food until it looked or smelled spoiled. We reused and repurposed everything: empty bottles, broken electronics, clothing. The economy of reusing and sharing seemed bigger than that of newly produced products.

By contrast, in America, there was just *so much* of everything. Watching my classmates move into their dorms with U-Haul trucks full of stuff, I realized that little repurposing was going on here. I had entered a land of plenty where certain people had plenty of everything. More than plenty.

"Durreen, I kept some pasta and sauce for you. Just go to the back and eat quickly before you start on the dishes," said Sophie as she busied herself refilling the coffeemaker. Sophie was an immigrant from Poland and in charge of the kitchen. She acted tough, but I knew she liked me. Her white uniform and white hair reminded me of Bubu. She, along with the rest of the kitchen staff, had become my family at Smith. They asked me how I was settling in and if I had enough warm clothes. I asked them about their kids and their bowling league.

Just like I found Bubu in Sophie, I found my elder sisters in the seniors in my house. By some wonderful mistake in the lottery, I found myself in a small single room, as the only first year on a floor full of seniors. So there I was, surrounded by a group of big sisters who shared their textbooks, notes, and profound wisdom on political science, philosophy, and history as well as wine, popcorn, pizza, and romance.

Living with the seniors also gave me special insight into the brewing activism on campus. Before long, I was being pulled, quickly and willingly, into heated debates around issues of racism, feminism, democracy, equality, and inclusion.

Once I helped plan a several-days-long protest against South African apartheid. As we went over the logistics of the takeover of College Hall, I had to be honest with the other planners. "I really want to be a part of this protest, but as a foreigner, I could be deported if I get arrested."

"Don't worry; we have you covered. We are not losing you," assured one woman, as the others frantically finished up our banners and speeches. Our demand was for Smith's endowment to divest from South Africa. All the books I had read by Miriam Tlali, Mafika Gwala, Andre Brink, and Nadine Gordimer had taught me about the injustice inflicted by the Afrikaaners and other white colonists on the native South Africans and other people of color. It had to be stopped, and I wanted to be a part of it. While literature and political pressure created awareness, I learned that the best way to make those in power feel pain was through economic pressure. Despite being on the other side of the world, we could put pressure on the apartheid government by forcing Smith College to divest from companies operating in South Africa.

So there we were, arm-in-arm outside the administrative building, chanting, "Divest from South Africa!" Soon sirens were blaring. It was a strange sight to see flashing lights of police cars in the quiet streets of the small college town of Northampton. We sat together on the cold ground, chanting away. As the protest wore on over several days, emotions ran high. Piles of snow on the ground and bone-chilling wind did not stop my brave Smith sisters from protesting. I was proud to be among them. Together we were learning firsthand the power of activism on financial markets.

Our discussions during the sit-in circled around change and power and money and justice. How could we most effectively convince Smith to divest? Wouldn't divestment hurt all South Africans, including people of color? But was there any other way to change things than to link investment to social change?

Key among our demands was that the Smith board of trustees issue a statement about divesting from South Africa, establish a divestment committee, and educate the trustees about apartheid. Another demand was amnesty for all students involved in the organized protest—a relief to all, especially us foreign students. It worked: Smith's board agreed to our demands and eventually decided to divest all $39 million they held in companies doing business in South Africa.

Smith's divestment movement ran parallel to those at other US universities, and our bold action opened up a world of possibilities for me. For the first time in my life, I saw the power of a social mission to move the financial markets and bring about real change. I realized the incredible weight of joining my own voice with the voices of others. What an exhilarating feeling.

Without knowing there would be a term for it in the future, university students had pushed our institutions toward socially responsible investing (SRI). SRI was the beginning of a movement to use investment decisions to combat environmental and social ills. Through SRI, investors withheld investment from companies producing tobacco, alcohol, and weapons; harming the environment; and promoting gambling. In this case, Smith stopped investing in companies doing business with a racially discriminatory regime. The student-led movement for divestment from South Africa became a poster child for SRI and a powerful reminder, for student activists and for others, that collective action could produce results.

Activism was exhilarating, my friends were kind, and my studies and work kept me busy. Yet even with all this support, I was homesick. I missed the warm sun, the taste of curry, the smell of Ma's jasmine perfume on her saris. Even when I was bone-tired, I would make myself work an extra hour so that I could make my once-a-month call to home last a minute longer. How could I explain my new life to my family halfway across the world? How could I even begin to explain the still undefined notions that were forming in my mind: about the power of financial markets and the possibility of using that power to correct some of the wrongs in the world?

CHAPTER SEVEN

Where Power Lives

The man in a sharp suit behind the reception desk looked me up and down. "Yes, how may I help you?" he asked. A low, condescending tone cut through his voice.

"I have a room reserved under my name," I said in measured tones. "Last name is Shahnaz: S-H-A-H-N-A-Z."

"Miss, are you *sure* you have a reservation at the Waldorf?" the man said doubtfully, his head cocked to the side.

I was wearing my usual jeans, sweater, and an ugly gray coat, which were the only winter clothes I could afford. Clearly the clerk thought I didn't belong here at the Waldorf Astoria, a fancy New York City hotel with marble floors and massive chandeliers. White people in expensive suits and dresses were mingling in the lobby.

I ignored his slight. "Yes, I do," I said calmly. "The bank I'm interviewing for reserved it. Now can you please check for my reservation?" I looked the man straight in the eye. He became flustered and looked for my name on his computer.

"Yes, I see it here. Welcome to the Waldorf Astoria." I took the key, smiled, and turned my head to nod at my brother, Isa, who had been making himself scarce behind a marble column.

We were getting used to this routine. This was my third trip, in the span of a few days, to New York City for a final round of job interviews. I had come to expect the same cold reception in all the hotels. I was the badly dressed woman of color with an accent who dared to ask for my room. Each time, the reaction of the hotel staff behind the desk was one of disbelief. Eventually, I started to have fun with it—as did Isa, who was staying with me for his spring break and accompanying me to New York for my interviews.

Isa had come to the United States to attend a private school in New Hampshire for his last two years of high school. I had orchestrated it for him. When my family returned to Bangladesh from the Philippines, Isa was having a tough time fitting back into the local school system. My parents mentioned that they were going to send him off to India for boarding school, something they could barely afford. They felt obliged to give their son a good high school education at any cost, and they didn't know what else to do.

I had heard from my Smith classmates about American boarding schools, so I got a list of top boarding schools on the East Coast and helped Isa apply. My parents were not thrilled with the idea, but they went along with it because they really did not think Isa would get in. Much to their surprise, Isa was not only accepted to Phillips Exeter Academy but offered both a full scholarship and round-trip plane tickets from Bangladesh.

So it was that, at age twenty, I became my fifteen-year-old brother's legal guardian. It was a role for which I had little preparation but which I had no choice but to embrace. All of a sudden I had another person to support and look after. The responsibility of keeping a teenage boy in line while ensuring that he makes the most of his opportunities at a top prep school in a foreign country: well, it was not what I wanted to take on. But it was my duty. This included having Isa stay with me in my dorm during his holidays. Having guests was against the rules, but my dorm mates looked the other way. And given my "in" with the kitchen staff, I could sneak out food for him at every meal.

Now I used my big-sister voice to tell Isa sternly that he had to stay in the hotel while I went to a pre-interview dinner. I couldn't afford to have something happen to him in New York, a city neither of us knew well. Isa wasn't happy, but he went back to eating his slice of pizza and watching TV.

With Isa safely settled in the hotel room, I decided to save on the taxi ride and walk to the Four Seasons, a restaurant frequented by people who worked on Wall Street. It was March and still very chilly, so I pulled the collar of my coat closer to my neck and walked faster to keep warm. I was not used to wearing heels, dresses, and pantyhose. It was all so constricting compared to my usual jeans, T-shirts, and sweaters.

Nearing the end of my college career, I was interviewing for positions at some of the largest investment banks, and my heart was full of questions. Was this the right path for me? Would it lead me to the power to enact real change by controlling the flow of money? Or had I lost my way? I didn't feel like I belonged in this Wall Street job-seeker group. I had classmates who had prepared for four years for these jobs, with the right summer internships at the right banks. Many of them had fathers who worked at these banks—or, better yet, who were the banks' clients. This was a wealthy man's world. Even the women had a particular Wall Street look: white, tall, and beautiful.

I had been accepted to the London School of Economics for a graduate degree in developmental economics: the study of how countries industrialize and become more wealthy. I had some money saved up, and I could have done a one-year master's program and then worked in the villages of Bangladesh to really help people. Maybe I'd just go through these interviews to get a taste of Wall Street. I wasn't going to get an offer anyway, I thought, as I walked to the restaurant. Who would want a girl from a poor country? My place was in Bangladesh.

But I wasn't convinced that development work could bring about systemic change or do away with the uneven power dynamics of the haves and have-nots. Would it make those who hold power give a damn about the powerless? During college, I had met countless economists in Washington, DC, people who worked at the World Bank and the International Monetary Fund. Not one of them had really solved economic disparities in the countries they served. Not one had brought respect and dignity to women and underserved communities. I thought of the women I knew growing up, most of whom had no options other than to marry. I had the chance to change that pattern here.

Maybe it was time to think about things differently, I thought to myself. Maybe I needed to learn the system that controls everything before I could dismantle it and change it to make it work for all. Then again, who was I to dare to take on the great financial systems of the world? My head was spinning. First, I had to get a job offer, I reminded myself as I walked into the restaurant; then I could think about these existential questions.

***

This is where power resides, I thought to myself as waiters ushered me to the Morgan Stanley group. I looked around at the tables covered in crisp, thick white tablecloths and set with perfect flower arrangements. As my eyes scanned the room, I noticed very few women and no women of color. I felt a pit in my stomach. Here we go.

The bankers who greeted me were friendly, white men with clean-cut Brooks Brothers looks. They cracked jokes effortlessly. The three men dining with me had all attended Ivy League universities and, as expected, the dreaded line came up. "Oh yes, you are from Smith," one of them said. "I went road tripping there all the time. You know the saying, right: Smith to bed, and Mount Holyoke to wed?"

Yes, I knew the line. After four years at Smith, a women's college that defined the feminist movement, I was familiar with the misogynistic reactions that Smith attracted. I steeled myself. If I was getting ready to jump in with the sharks, I had better know how to keep my cool and use humor as my weapon.

The drinks flowed, and the menu came. I knew from the career office that I should order something easy to eat, something not too messy. This way I could engage in the conversation instead of being distracted by the food.

"Durreen, you order the wine," one of the men directed me. I knew it was a test. I had expected something like this, and I had asked my friends at the dorm to give me a rundown on wines, as I knew nothing about them. "With chicken and fish, you need to order a white wine. With red meat and red sauce, a red wine," they told me. "The safest is to order a Chardonnay: ask for a dry one, and California is the best bet. "

"Shall we try a dry Chardonnay?" I said, then turned to the waiter and asked, "What would you recommend? The list looks fantastic." Of course, I knew none of the dozens of wines on the list.

The waiter recommended a Chilean wine. "Fabulous! I love Chilean wine," I said, although I had never had any. "They are so wonderfully unpredictable." I could tell my tablemates were impressed. They were looking for someone confident, and I was faking confidence very well. Inside I was dying of nervousness.

***

Within weeks I had six job offers at banks in New York and Boston, all willing to go through the trouble of sponsoring my work visa. My friends at Smith thought I had lost my mind. Why would I want to work on Wall Street? they asked. Wasn't I a torch-bearing liberal who wanted to save the world? Was I already selling my soul?

"If you want to change the system, you need to know how it works," I told them. "Why does so much power lie in this financial system? Who controls it?" My friends rolled their eyes, convinced I was compromising the values we'd defended together for years.

My parents disapproved of my choice as well, but for a different reason. They wanted me to earn a graduate degree and then return home so they could arrange a marriage for me. But I simply had no intention of returning until I had the tools I needed to change the financial system, empower women, and empower myself.

I also earned the vitriol of the women who had been preparing for banking jobs for four years. I frequently heard whispers behind my back on campus that spring. "It's so unfair she got all these offers," I'd hear someone whisper. "Well, you know she only got them because of the diversity quota," another would say.

Sometimes, when I'd hear a conversation like that, I'd turn around calmly, smile, and say, "I'm sorry that you did not receive the job offers you wanted. But I didn't take the offers from you. I got the offers because I deserved them. Firms have to go through a lot of legal hoops to hire me, as a foreign student. So I guess I am really good and they wanted me very badly." Yes, it was blunt, but these women needed to hear that I had gotten these job offers on my own. I was tired of their sense of entitlement.

I proudly accepted the job offer from Morgan Stanley. Decades earlier Morgan Stanley had started a financial analyst program with six Smith graduates as an entry-level route for women to join the ranks of Wall Street. I was happy to continue the Smith tradition.

At our graduation ceremony, the famous economist Kenneth Galbraith gave the commencement speech. He spoke at length about the evils of Wall Street and how young minds were being destroyed by the pursuit of wealth. My friends turned around to look at me, shook their heads, and in good-natured teasing, mouthed, "He's talking about you!"

Fine, I thought, with a smile; let my friends and an icon of American liberalism mock me. I had my own plans that, while vague, included figuring out a way to change an unfair economic system that disadvantaged women who looked like me. To do that, I had to figure out how the mechanisms of finance worked. So there I was, a college graduate with an impossible dream and a family halfway around the world, headed straight into the engine of global power.

After the ceremony, I looked around and saw the happy faces of my friends and their families hugging and kissing, tears rolling down their cheeks. I was happy for them. My time at Smith, a college that helped me find my voice, was over. I walked back alone to my room in the empty dorm, sat on my bed, and cried.

I cried tears of happiness, for getting a degree that had seemed so unreachable for me. I cried tears of sadness because I had nobody to share this moment with. I cried tears of fear, not knowing what lay ahead. Deep down, however, I knew that this journey was the right one. I hoped it would benefit not only me but the millions of women in the world who have no opportunity to come this close to the source of power.

CHAPTER EIGHT

Off to Wall Street

I was late. It was 9:10 a.m., and I was hyperventilating at the reception desk of the Exxon building in midtown Manhattan. The security guard handed me my pass and shook her head. "Late on your first day!" she said. I slipped into the crowded elevator just as the doors were closing. The twenty-sixth-floor button on the panel was already lit, so someone else was going there too. I hoped it wasn't anyone important. As the elevator stopped on what seemed like every floor to let off passengers, I became more anxious. My anxiety must have been obvious, because a man's voice next to me said calmly, "Relax. We'll get there on time."

I looked at the suit beside me, and as my eyes traveled up, they landed on a very handsome face that looked like Clark Kent's, the mild-mannered alter ego of Superman, behind a pair of not very flattering eyeglasses. The man was about six feet tall, very fit, with dark hair and kind blue eyes. I was tongue-tied. "I hope so," I said.

As soon as the elevator door opened, we jogged toward the conference room, where the orientation was already underway. "Don't worry," my new colleague said. "I am sure we can sneak in the back."

Clark Kent was wrong. We had to walk up to the front of the room, past about sixty people, to take the last two available seats. In the front row.

"One thing you need to learn is not to be late on your first day," the president of Morgan Stanley said, looking straight at the two of us. "Sorry," I mouthed. Meanwhile, Clark Kent didn't seem flustered at all. How could he be so confident? Clearly, he looked like he belonged here, and I didn't. But still.

The speeches continued. An African American vice president, one of the only two Black people in the room, told us plainly that for the next two years we belonged to the bank. We were the cream of the crop, and we had been chosen because we were the smartest, most hard working, and best looking. The crowd laughed. "You will be walking through hallways of power. You need to know how to handle the power that will be bestowed upon you," he continued. We could not talk to anyone about the transactions we would be working on. If we did, we might be implicated for insider trading, a crime involving trading stocks based on information not publicly available. The year before, a financial analyst just like us had been arrested when he shared what he was working on with his girlfriend, whose family then traded shares of the client company.

He also stressed that we would be expected to work hard—very hard, as in "pulling all-nighters" hard. With these long hours would come frustration, hurt, and anger. We might work for obnoxious or insensitive people. "If you feel like crying, go to the restroom, flush the toilet, and cry there," he said. "Nobody here is interested in your tears."

We were each given a beeper—this was before cell phones—and were told to treat it as a part of ourselves for the next two years. We would need to carry them with us everywhere, even to the bathroom. We were told that three groups of people in New York deal with life and death and therefore wear beepers: doctors, drug dealers, and Morgan Stanley bankers.

I sat there trying to absorb speech after speech. Power and fear appeared to be two sides of the same coin. In overcoming fear, one obtains power; over time, if not checked, this power turns into hubris. Was overcoming fear success? Or was it obtaining power? How much of success was due to fear of failure versus hubris of power? I wasn't sure which side was up. What in the world had I gotten myself into?

When the break time came, Clark Kent turned to me and held out his hand. "Hi, I'm Robert Kraybill. That was quite a walk of shame for us wasn't it?"

"Yes, not a great start," I said, introducing myself. He seemed sweet, but I was distracted, lost in a sea of smart, good-looking men and women in their early twenties, all eager to start the race to make money. Everyone looked confident, at ease, and as though they were born to do this. In the entire class of sixty, there were only a dozen women and only three or four people of color.

My new peers seemed years ahead of me. Many of them had undergraduate degrees in business or had already worked on Wall Street as interns. They already knew how to navigate the system. Conversation whizzed around me. "Yeah, I popped in a few weeks ago and met with the groups I want to work in . . . " "I have been practicing how to create a leveraged buyout financial model from scratch!" "My dad called up his buddy here and put in a word for me—you know, the horse-trading has already started."

My head throbbed; it was all too much. What were these people even talking about? They were strategizing their fast-track Wall Street careers, and I had just figured out how to put on a skirt suit.

***

"Wayne, I have no idea how to do this leveraged buyout model." I turned to the second-year analyst whose desk was right behind mine. "Any chance you can help me out?"

"Nope, sorry. I have plans." With that, Wayne left for the day, disappearing down the hallway—along with my chances of getting any sleep that night. It was 9:00 p.m.; I was utterly exhausted, and I had no idea where to start. After working sixteen- to eighteen-hour days, day after day, I could no longer tell whether I was physically exhausted from lack of sleep or mentally exhausted from dealing with new concepts under incredible time pressure. Or both. All I knew was that I was bone-tired. I longed to lie down on the floor, curl up, and take a nap.

Following that orientation session, our entire class had taken part in a two-week "mini-MBA" training program at Columbia University. After that, we were thrown into the ocean of investment banking to see if we could swim. Not only did we need to start racing immediately, we also needed to know many different strokes. This meant not only understanding finance and accounting but also being proficient in the financial modeling software of the time. We had to know some programming so that we could write macros to fill in the holes in what were still very early versions of desktop software. To print trading graphs, we had to master a cumbersome proprietary data analysis system. Presentation slides had to be drawn and written out by hand, before being entrusted to the word processing department, which had access to specialized design software. Decades later, these tasks would become much easier for Wall Street underlings thanks to Microsoft Office and the proliferation of Bloomberg terminals. But in those days, you learned very quickly that without an ecosystem of friends, you would not swim very far or very fast. Thankfully, our class had started to bond, through work and play, and I now had friends across departments: mergers and acquisitions, debt capital markets, equity capital markets, treasury, and others.

Yet that was just one-half of the ecosystem. Unlike many of my peers, I nurtured relationships with the support staff as well, the majority of whom were people of color like myself. Their families hailed from all over—China, Guatemala, Haiti, Mexico, Uganda, the Philippines, and many other countries. I developed a good rapport with the receptionists, the word processing team, and the photocopiers—not because I had to but because I wanted to. They were the invisible people in the bank, and yet without them, the work would not get done. I liked them as friends, and I wanted them to know how much I appreciated their work. They all came from the New York I craved to be a part of in some way. I felt comfortable with them, and I found our exchanges refreshing. These were the real New Yorkers who could not access the power of high finance but who kept our bank running day in day out.

***

"Durreen, where the fuck are you?" The vice president in our group was screaming from her office at the top of her voice. Natalie's office was ten feet away from the "bullpen," where the analysts sat, so when she yelled—which was often and usually directed at me—our whole side of the floor heard.

It was ten in the morning on the day after I had been asked to prepare my first leveraged buyout model. After Wayne had left me in the lurch, my dear friend Mona, who had graduated from Smith a year before me and was now a second-year analyst in another department, had guided me through it. I had completed it in time to present it at an 8:00 a.m. meeting and had just returned from that meeting. I was just getting my head around the follow-up work that was required when Natalie's scream pierced my sleep-deprived mind.

I ran down the hall to Natalie's office. As I stood at her door, she looked me up and down and let out the smoke from her cigarette. "I don't know what savage country you are from," she said in a low voice, "but in this country, we shower and we wear shoes."

Natalie insulted me openly all the time, and I was beginning to develop some immunity to it. I was also learning how to counter it through humor. Yes, I had just pulled an all-nighter and had been wearing the same clothes for twenty-four hours. Yes, I did look disheveled. And yes, I was barefoot, as it's impossible to wear heels for twenty-four hours straight. Having jumped up from my desk to respond to Natalie's scream, I had forgotten to put my heels back on.

I smiled. "Showers? Shoes? Sleep? Nope, don't know what they are. We don't have them in my country. But, hey, I would not mind a pair of your Ferragamos." I eyed the pile of designer shoes boxes in the corner of her office.

"Good try. Where the fuck is my work?"

"I haven't finished it yet; I have been killing myself on the other deal."

"Well, I don't care," she said. "I need it ASAP!"

I walked back to my desk. This is what my life has come to: pulling all-nighters to get my work done and being yelled at for doing so. But I was getting closer to the power, right?

Just when I thought the day could not get worse, Isa called from Exeter. "I can't talk now, Isa. But is everything OK?"

"I'm fine," he said. "I'm just calling to let you know as my guardian that a group of us from Exeter are taking a bus to Pennsylvania to support the antinuclear movement and protest at Three Mile Island." A decade earlier, in 1979, the Three Mile Island accident had demonstrated the dangers of nuclear power to the American public when one of its reactors suffered a partial meltdown. The incident had created ripples of fear, which had spawned calls for stricter nuclear safety regulation and led to antinuclear energy protests. Now a group of large utility companies was seeking financing to rebuild the melted reactors, leading to public outrage.

I sighed as I listened to Isa's plan. In a rather incredible turn of events, financing for the utility companies was one of the deals I was working on at that precise moment. In the span of four short years, I had gone from protesting companies investing in apartheid South Africa to now enabling the financing of a nuclear power plant with serious public safety issues. I had raised my concerns about nuclear power in one of the meetings about our financing of the utility companies' plan to rebuild, but my challenge had been firmly dismissed. We were expected to shut up and do the work we were hired to do. This was the dark side of finance, and I was slowly being sucked into it.

"Yes, you should definitely go and protest," I told Isa. "But be safe, OK?" With that, I hung up. I couldn't say anything more. I was closer than ever to the bastion of power, yet it was a strange and disempowering kind of proximity. I felt the power of my words to impact people positively or negatively, to move the market, even to land me in jail for insider trading. I couldn't say a word.

Is this what I wanted? Yes, my work created value in the world, but primarily for a single stakeholder: the shareholders. I knew that the people who own shares in a company are far from the only people impacted by that company. What about the other stakeholders—customers, employees, communities, families, the environment? How did they get compensated for the company's impact on them—and why didn't the market measure or value that impact?

All these factors felt deeply intertwined with risk. If the owners of the power plant had thought about all their stakeholders, perhaps they could have avoided the meltdown of the nuclear plant and subsequent outcry. As the bankers bringing financing to this company, we didn't seem to be factoring all the issues into our analysis.

***

"So you are going to let them win?" Rob asked me over dinner one evening. We were at a sushi restaurant on the ground floor of the Exxon building, where Morgan Stanley had several floors, before heading back to our desks to work. I was recounting my recent episodes with him and shared that I was thinking of quitting.

"In their eyes, I can't do anything right," I said. "What is the point? It has been three months of hell. Do you know they even pick on what I wear? I wore a pair of culottes with a jacket, and I was sent to HR and then sent home to change. I was told this is a bank, and women cannot wear pants of any kind. Really?"

"I don't know about fashion, but I do think you get a lot more grief than others do," Rob said. He was not the first person to notice, and I was grateful each time a colleague commented on the blatant gender and race discrimination. Being a woman, especially a woman of color, was not easy in a macho, white-male atmosphere, and it was my friends who made the job bearable.

Each day I was getting closer to Rob. He was quiet and tended not to join in the group from the office who went out for dinners and dancing. When we began dating, I kept it quiet at work, letting only a few close friends know. I was also careful to keep the relationship secret from my South Asian friends and acquaintances. The South Asian community was a more efficient news network than Reuters, and I didn't want the news to get back to my parents, who had told me repeatedly not to date an American.

This all changed the night of the office Christmas party, which was the biggest event of the year. On the night of the party, I was exhausted from another week with little sleep, and I had not found time to eat the whole day. So the marvelous food and free-flowing drinks at a downtown club were a welcome release. I drank a lot, danced some, and ate little. I was feeling very tipsy when I saw Rob walking toward me: Superman in a tuxedo! I stopped. My heart stopped. He was so handsome. Before I knew what I was doing, I had run up to him, thrown my arms around his neck, and kissed him. For a long time. He smiled. Everyone had stopped what they were doing and stared at us, but I didn't care.

When I walked into the office the next morning, I knew I was in trouble. "Well, that was quite a show you put on," a colleague said. "They are waiting for you in the managing director's office."

The entire senior management team of my group was waiting for me. I was asked to sit down, and then the admonishment started. How dare I behave like a "whore"? Did I not know how a banker should behave? The criticisms came from all directions. I listened and tried to take it all in.

Finally, gathering myself, I began asking questions. I tried to keep my voice calm and level. Would they have said this to me if I were a man, I asked? Would kissing my white boyfriend have bothered them if I weren't a brown woman? Which was worse: me kissing my boyfriend in public or a managing director sleeping with the female underlings in private?

Silence filled the room. With that, I stood up and left. I knew it wasn't the end of anything, but for the moment, I had won the battle for myself, for women, and for people of color.

Shaking with fury and revulsion, I called Rob and asked if he had received the same treatment in his department.

He was surprised. "Are you joking? Everyone was high-fiving me when I walked in."

CHAPTER NINE

Balancing between Two Worlds

The chaos of Dhaka airport hits you as hard as the hot, humid air of the city: people yelling, porters grabbing for your suitcase, police trying to control the crowd with their batons. It was strange to see a sea of people in sarongs and kurta pajamas instead of the blue suits that I had gotten used to in New York. At this moment, New York and Dhaka felt like two entirely separate worlds, neither one knowing or caring about the other's existence.

My parents had called me only a few days earlier to tell me of my third sister's imminent wedding. "What do you mean Tazneen is getting married in three days?" I had exclaimed.

"Well, she threatened to elope. First a love affair, and now this! We had no choice but to agree to the wedding. Who would have thought this sweet, pretty daughter of mine would end up bringing so much shame to the family?" Ma's voice trailed away. Even across the twelve-thousand-mile phone connection, I could hear her bitter disappointment.

"Ma, she is not bringing shame. She loves Jalal," I protested.

"Don't talk to me like an American! We are not Americans," Ma retorted. "We have our own traditions. We pick the man who we know will be best for each of our daughters. We chose husbands for your two elder sisters, and they have no complaints. Nothing can be arranged now except for a quick wedding."

At the airport, I sighed in relief when I saw Tazneen weaving through the crowd toward me. It was my first trip back to Bangladesh in several years. Since then, I had finally settled in at Morgan Stanley. I could understand market trends, the company's unique nuances, and the financing mechanisms that raised hundreds of millions of dollars for growth or acquisitions of companies. I had developed a thick skin to cope with the toxic environment. I was quick on my feet, I could play with the numbers, and I was confident in my abilities.

Tazneen was clearly agitated by the stress of her impending wedding. I was proud of her for standing up for what she wanted, but I could see it was taking a toll. On the ride to our childhood home from the airport, I took in the sights of Dhaka. Construction sites spilled onto the road, combining with potholes to form an obstacle course for the cars, motorbikes, buses, trucks, rickshaws, auto-rickshaws, and occasional roaming cows that all shared the overburdened thoroughfares. Fumes from the exhaust pipes of automobiles choked the air. There were no crossings other than an occasional overhead pedestrian bridge that looked so run down that most people preferred the risk of just darting across the road. Yet despite the dust, fumes, and traffic congestion, the city was transforming. The sleepy vibe of the Dhaka of my childhood had been replaced by the rush of a city eager to catch up but not really knowing how.

As our car came alongside a park, I noticed a group of children with torn clothes and dirty faces. They were sitting on the pavement under the shade of a banyan tree, weaving garlands of jasmine. When the car stopped at the traffic light, two little girls cut through the lanes of traffic, tapped on our window, smiling and holding up the jasmine garlands. This was entrepreneurship in its purest form. I thought of my stamp trading from long ago, and I knew I had to support them.

I turned to Tazneen, who was already smiling and pulling out a twenty-taka note. Our mother had taught us to help every single entrepreneur, no matter how small.

I rolled down the window and paid for two garlands. Then I turned to Tazneen and pinned one in her hair. "Now you look like a bride," I said. She smiled, and I could see her relief that I was home.

***

The actual Muslim wedding ceremony is a simple affair, with the groom sitting in one room with the men and the bride sitting in another with the women. The imam first asks the bride if she wants to marry and then he asks the groom. Then both parties sign the wedding certificate. Tazneen's wedding was taking place at home, and she sat in the middle of the bed in my parents' bedroom in a beautiful red silk sari with her head covered. I could see the anxiety in her eyes and the sparkle of excitement. As a bride, she was supposed to keep her eyes downcast, but Tazneen's eyes were darting all around the room. The room, full of my aunts and female cousins.

Just then, my mother sent for me from the veranda. "Ma, what is it? I took care of everything. You need to be with Tazneen. The ceremony will start any moment."

"Thank you. Yes, I will go in, but I need you to stay out here," she explained. "Your father is so upset about this wedding that he is having chest pain. He won't attend the ceremony. Stay with him in case he becomes really sick."

"Ma, you must be joking! This is ridiculous. You know Papa is faking it. He is annoyed about the wedding and is using this as an excuse not to attend the ceremony."

"I don't know if he is faking it, and neither do you. Do you want to have your father have a heart attack during the wedding ceremony?"

I was livid, but there was nothing I could do. I plopped down on one of the wicker chairs in the veranda as my father came and joined me. He looked upset but didn't seem to be in physical pain. "So, are you really having chest pains?" I asked with little sympathy, as I heard the rooms inside quieting down and the wedding ceremony starting.

"I am not feeling well," my father said in a low voice. He was stooped over and focused intently on his hands as he did whenever he was thinking hard. He was quiet.

"You know the wedding ceremony is going on inside now," I said, hoping to convince him to go in.

"I know. I am very sad about this wedding." As he said this, he took my hand, looked me straight in the eyes, and said, "Promise me that you will not bring such shame to our family. I won't be able to take another shock like this."

I did not know what to say. If I told him the truth—that not only was I intent on avoiding an arranged marriage but was actually dating a white American in New York—he might actually have had a heart attack, right there and then. All I could muster was, "I will do my best."

I heard cheering inside then and knew that the wedding ceremony had ended. Tazneen was married. I had missed it, and my father had avoided his own daughter's wedding because he wanted to flex his power. In my head, I thought, "Well, wait until you see what comes next. If you think you have power, you have it wrong." Outwardly, I sighed, patted his hand, and calmly whispered, "Your daughter just got married. Be happy for her. Give her your blessings."

It was a good thing I was leaving for New York the next day.

***

One evening shortly after my trip to Bangladesh, when I came back late to our apartment, my roommate Jean was glued to the television. Flashing on the screen were horrifying images of a storm: winds blowing, huge angry waves crashing on land, vast scenes of devastation. I saw women in saris and men in sarongs walking through waist-deep floodwater, sorting through waterlogged items and precariously balancing children on their arms and possessions on top of their heads.

"Jean, what is happening? Where is this?"

"I'm so sorry, Durreen," she said. "This is Bangladesh. There has been a terrible cyclone. The reports are saying the storm was one of the worst in history. It's still going on. The storm surge was twenty feet. They're saying the death toll may be close to 150,000. Over 10 million people have lost everything."

I sat down next to her, speechless. I couldn't fathom the level of devastation or imagine how my country could take on any more suffering. It felt like we'd go forward four steps, only to have politics or nature take us back three. I had to call home.

After more than an hour of trying to get through, at last I heard the phone ringing on the other side and then Ma's tired, worried voice, "Hello?"

"Ma, are you OK? Is everyone OK?"

"We're OK, but this is a bad one. We haven't experienced anything like this since 1970, when we had ninety-foot tidal waves and over half a million people died." Her voice trailed off. We talked some more, and after we hung up, I sat there holding the phone and rocking back and forth. I needed to do something.

The next day, an article about the storm appeared on the front page of the *New York Times*: "BANGLADESH CYCLONE KILLS OVER 150,000 PEOPLE." Reading the article on the subway on the way to work, I looked up and saw the other subway riders going about their daily lives. A mother was balancing a toddler on her lap, a corporate type in a suit was reading a skillfully folded newspaper while holding onto a hanging strap for balance, and a construction worker, ready with his hard hat, was balancing himself without holding onto anything.

We are all constantly balancing ourselves in life, I thought. I felt the sudden sense that I needed to rebalance my life. I needed to tip it in the direction of the things I cared most deeply about. I needed to connect my worlds and I had an idea.

When I got to work, I went straight to human resources and described my plan: creating a flyer with facts about the cyclone in Bangladesh and details about how employees could donate to a nonprofit to support relief work. My plea to HR worked. I could send an appeal to every single employee of the company in North America. I wrote a personal note about how, as bankers, we have a responsibility toward both economic systems and humanity. My friends in the graphics department helped me design it, and my friends at the mail center helped me make several thousand copies and stuff the envelopes.

The first day passed, and only the usual memos and circulars appeared in my inbox. Same with the second day. My heart started to sink. But then, on the third day, the envelopes started trickling in with checks of varying amounts: $50, $100, $250. It looked like I might be able to raise $5,000 or so for the cyclone relief effort.

At that point the big checks started coming in—$2,500, $5,000— and I recognized the names. These were the managing directors, generally thought to be a coldhearted bunch. Somehow the letter had touched them, and they were writing checks. The checks kept pouring in. I even received a $10,000 check with a note from a managing director in Chicago: "Durreen, this is the first time I have seen an analyst take it upon herself to help a group of people on the other side of the world. I commend your effort and wish you all the best."

I couldn't believe it. That generous check took me to $60,000 for the relief and rebuilding efforts in Bangladesh. I felt grateful and proud of bankers and friends who had all pulled through for me. All it took was a letter. Maybe they weren't heartless after all.

I wrote thank-you letters to every single person who had donated and told them how the organization we donated to would use the money. How easy it had been to make a bridge, no matter how tenuous or temporary, between my two worlds! How intuitive it felt to make power work for the powerless, and to tip the scale even slightly from the superrich 1 percent to the 99 percent.

Rebalancing my life felt right. After years of trying to simply survive a challenging work environment, I was finding my purpose again.

***

"Rob, I am thinking of going back to Bangladesh," I blurted out. We were walking around Greenwich Village after dinner at our favorite little French bistro. Rob stopped in his tracks.

"What? Why? Is this because of my mother?"

I had met Rob's mother on a recent weekend visit to her house in New Jersey, and it had been a disaster. Rob had failed to tell his mother that I wasn't white until about ten minutes before she had met me. The weekend had ended with Betty sending Rob out on errands while she sat me down at the kitchen table to give me some advice. "Listen, Durreen, I am sure you are a fine young woman, but you need to go back to your country," she told me. "You don't belong here. You don't belong with Rob. You have nothing in common. You are from a different race and religion. It will never work!" Betty had lit a cigarette and was looking straight into my eyes. "You are young; you will soon forget about each other. You have arranged marriages in your culture, right? You should go home and let your parents find you a husband. They know what is best for you."

"You know that she will come around," Rob was saying now. "Why would you just leave? Is it me?" He was visibly upset and agitated.

"No, it is not about your mother," I said. "It is not about you, and it is not about my parents or culture. It is about me, and about what I want to do. I love New York and our time together, but it is time for me to go home."

Fighting back tears, I went on. "You know I came to work at Morgan Stanley with one goal: to learn about financial markets to take that knowledge back to help others. Now I want to build a bridge from this world of economic elites to the millions who don't even know what Wall Street is."

I knew my plan sounded idealistic, but I had to keep rebalancing my work and my values. I had to bring power back with me to those I cared about, I told him. When I raised money for the survivors of that cyclone, it felt right. I loved Rob, but I couldn't ignore what increasingly felt like a calling.

I focused on distant streetlights while I talked, not daring to look at Rob because I would start crying. He was silent, and the noise of the street was blocked out, as all my senses focused on Rob. What was he thinking? Why wasn't he saying anything? I could feel my body tensing up.

Then I felt a squeeze on my hand. "I understand," he said quietly. "You do what you have to do. I will be here for you." An incredible sense of relief washed over me.

My conversation with the HR department resulted in pushback as well. "What? You want to go back to Bangladesh?" an incredulous HR employee exclaimed. "You are doing so well here. Why would you throw all that away?"

It was tempting to give in to common sense. Yes, I was at the pinnacle, and I was walking away from it. But, yes, I knew I was making the right decision. "I really appreciate the offer to stay on," I said. "It means a lot, but I need to return home to use the amazing things I learned here back in Bangladesh."

"But there is no Wall Street in Bangladesh," she said. "Do you know that you are the first Bangladeshi woman to work on Wall Street? We found that out when we applied for your work visa." No, I hadn't known that. She kept on pressing. "You can do so much more if you stay on. Think of the money, if nothing else! Wouldn't you rather earn money and donate it rather than go back and dig ditches yourself?"

No, there was no Wall Street or Morgan Stanley in Bangladesh. But there were 60 million women—women whose lives I could impact by trying to connect them to what Wall Street had to offer. I wanted to do something to create a better and inclusive world today, not tomorrow. My younger self balked at donating rice to the poor week after week; how would donating money be any different? I wanted to change the world today, with my passion and skills, not tomorrow, with my money.

So I donated my fancy work clothes to the Salvation Army, hoping they would help other women break into the corporate world. The rest of my things fit in a single box, which I left with Rob. A beautiful silk scarf Rob had given me on my birthday caught my eye as I was packing. I bunched it up in my fist, closed my eyes, and inhaled its smell. It smelled of my life in New York, which was coming to an end.

Rob arrived at my apartment to take me to the airport as I was fitting the last items into my suitcase. I had come to America with one suitcase, and I was leaving with two. Yet I was leaving behind so many things I had acquired and treasured over the past six years: my freedom, my voice, and the man I loved. I was taking home with me a knowledge of finance and a passion to use that knowledge to do good, packed away in the extra baggage of idealism.

CHAPTER TEN

Cross the Bridge

"This work will require you to stay in remote villages. To reach them, you will need to take a public bus and then, when that drops you off, a bullock cart, a rickshaw, or even a dinghy. You will need to stay with the field staff, who are mostly men, in the staff quarters—which are Spartan, to say the least. After your life in New York, I'm assuming that all this will come as a shock."

It was the fall of 1991, near the end of the monsoon season, and Professor Mohammad Yunus, the founder of what was at the time a small but innovative bank, was introducing me to my new job. The bank provided microloans—less than fifty dollars—to rural women starting businesses in our native Bangladesh. Fifteen years later, Yunus and the bank he founded—Grameen Bank—would share the Nobel Peace Prize for their revolutionary work in bringing women and underserved communities into the banking sector.

Right now, though, he was patiently lecturing me with a knowing smile and a twinkle in his eyes. Yunus wore his trademark cotton *fatua*, a traditional Bengali shirt. We were sitting in his sparse office in front of bookshelves spilling over with thick tomes on economics. Traffic noise from the street traveled in on a gentle breeze through the window. Despite the breeze and the ceiling fan, sweat was dripping down my body. I was no longer used to the heat and humidity or to being wrapped in the traditional five yards of cloth of a sari.

"And the work itself: well, after Wall Street, the work will appear monotonous and mundane," he was telling me. "Your clients were Fortune 500 companies. Now your clients will be poor, rural women who have no education, are unable to send their children to school, and consider themselves lucky if they can get two meals a day. You will need to explain to your new clients—and their husbands—how a loan from Grameen Bank can enable them to build a new future for themselves and their families."

In the Grameen Bank model, women form a group of five and act as each other's guarantors for a loan. The group's trust, support, and peer pressure take the place of the expensive collateral that other banks would require. Each member of the group receives a loan as well as training in a variety of topics, such as how to save money and how to start a small business.

Before Grameen came along and offered them tiny loans directly, these women had no opportunity to deal with money until they were pulled into it due to a personal crisis, such as a male family member's death or illness. With a small loan from Grameen, women could take baby steps toward financial independence by starting an income-generating activity, such as buying a cow and selling its milk or weaving fishing nets.

An economist by training, Yunus was one of the pioneers of this novel method of economic development: providing access to very small loans in underserved rural communities. He saw the limitation of traditional philanthropy and donations and focused on financial empowerment through small loans to the women. The concept, known as microcredit, had been experimented with in India and the Philippines. But Yunus's innovative practice of group lending, where the group of women acted as guarantors for each other, would help Grameen Bank become the most visible early success in the new field.

I turned my attention back to Professor Yunus's words. I could use my finance skills more effectively at Standard Chartered Bank, he was telling me. Our country lacked professionals with the level of finance training that I had, and I could put it to use there. But I was undeterred. The more he tried to dissuade me, the more eager I became to work at Grameen. Yes, this was the other end of the financial spectrum than I had experienced, but this was exactly what I had come home for. Finding ways to make finance work for the 99 percent was becoming my way to defy a system that disenfranchised so many. Grameen fit the bill so well.

"With all due respect, Sir, I understand that it won't be easy," I said. "But I want to do it, and I know Grameen will find my skills useful. You need capital to grow Grameen Bank, and I can help you access that capital from the market." Pausing, I saw that he was intrigued and more attentive. "I know how to do it, so please let me help you."

Professor Yunus smiled. I knew by the look on his face that at last I had convinced him.

***

Weeks later, balancing on a bamboo bridge fifteen feet above the rushing water of an overflowing canal, I began to wonder whether Yunus was right. The bridge consisted of two strips of bamboo: a single length of bamboo to walk on, and another one as a handrail. As I looked down, trying to find a grip on the slippery bamboo with my equally slippery flip-flops, I watched water rushing with all its might through the narrow channel below me. "I can do this," I kept repeating while taking tiny, careful steps, one foot in front of the other.

I had been placed in the planning and monitoring department, where my skills in financial analysis and strategic planning would be of most use. The bank was beginning to experience loan defaults at certain centers. All banks expect a certain number of defaults, but my task was to understand why and how borrowers were defaulting on their loans and then develop a plan, backed by a financial model, to return those centers to profitability. I needed to figure out how to make individual bank branches more profitable, possibly by offering different kinds of loans and cutting down on management costs. I would also figure out how to involve Grameen in more profit-generating projects, such as fisheries and agriculture. I'd work with a few village centers as models and sources of data and then, from there, develop the financial model for the next five years for the bank.

I had arrived in the area early the previous morning on a public bus, which had welcomed me with its ripped seats with foam spilling out, windows with broken glass or no glass at all, and floor covered with red betel nut juice. A Grameen colleague had greeted me at the dusty bus stop and walked me to the next step of my journey. "*Apa*, here is our ride," my colleague said, addressing me as "Sister," a respectful way of addressing a woman who is not a relative. He led me over to a bullock cart with a bamboo bed parked nearby. So there I was, in a cart pulled by a tired old bull, through the rural town center to one of Grameen Bank's village offices. The wooden wheels turned slowly on the muddy paths, jarring every muscle of my body each time they slid from rut to rut. Eventually, the bullock cart stopped in front of a mud hut with a tin roof and the red and green Grameen Bank sign on a shingle in front.

My colleague showed me to the room where I would be staying. There I found a wooden bed frame covered with a woven traditional *pati*, a mat woven from dry palm leaves, and a stained pillow. Folded on the corner of the bed lay a mosquito net, and on the floor was a kerosene lamp.

We ate meals sitting on the floor—rice and lentils most days, and if we were lucky, a vegetable and a piece of fish. Our three meals a day were a luxury from the perspective of the villagers we served. Food was always precious and scarce, especially during the monsoon season, when little grew due to excessive rain.

I was the only woman among the bank staff, which wasn't much different than my time on Wall Street. My colleagues here had little exposure to the outside world. They had spent their lives growing up in small villages like the one we were in now. But they believed deeply in our work at Grameen, and they took incredible pride in the role they were playing in developing our country.

I was happy to be among people who did not define their existence by how much money they made or what Ivy League university they had attended, but rather by a sense of duty and service. My new colleagues knew I came from overseas, but they did not ask me many questions; that life in the United States was simply too foreign. They were respectful of me and my work with them, and that was what I needed.

My assignment in the bank was not going to be easy: learning why some centers were experiencing high levels of unpaid loans while others were doing well and then using these insights to grow the bank and help more women. First, however, I had to make it across the bamboo bridge.

Everything about village life becomes doubly difficult during the rainy season, when the monsoon comes to the Indian subcontinent with all its rage and grace. Some days the rain is so fierce it's like steel bullets are pelting down from the sky. Other days the rain drizzles gently for hours on end, leaving everything shining, sparkling, and so very slippery.

The rain had paused for now, but the bamboo bridge was slick. A group of young boys jumped from the edge of the canal bank to watch me, pointing and laughing. I didn't want to be their circus act, so I focused on one small step at a time, one foot in front of the other, and eventually made it to the other side.

They ran over to me. "You made it! We thought you were going to fall!" one boy exclaimed in Bengali village dialect. "You should run across the bamboo bridge like we do." Another ran easily across on his bare feet to demonstrate.

"Well, now I know," I said with a weak smile. "Do you know where the Nikhilgram village is? I need to go there to meet some women."

"We are from Nikhilgram. Why are you coming to our village? You don't look or sound like you're from a village, and you don't have your head covered!"

The boys walked me through muddy paddy fields, along narrow pathways forming borders between neighboring rice fields. More than 120 million people in a country the size of Wisconsin means that land is the most precious commodity. And the land keeps getting divided into smaller and smaller plots across generations, making it next to impossible to make a living as a farmer. In this context, small loans for women to start-up their own businesses allow families to begin to break the shackles of poverty.

The boys and I walked for several miles in the rain, which had started up again. Finally, we arrived at an enclave of mud huts surrounded by banana, mango, and jackfruit trees. In the middle of the huts stood an elevated clay platform, covered with a thatched roof, which served as a community gathering area. A group of men wearing sarongs stood on one side, most of them bare-chested and the remainder wearing undershirts. On the other side stood a group of women, their heads covered with the ends of their saris.

Walking closer, I saw that the men were holding sickles and machetes in their hands. I also noticed two of my Grameen colleagues were already there. They were standing with the armed men and, frankly, looking terrified.

I quickly realized that I needed to defuse the situation. I didn't yet fully understand what was going on, but I had a guess. Women who create a second source of income not only bring economic relief to their families; they also empower themselves. Not all men in our traditional society welcome this change. New earnings from their wives might be a boon to the household, but they still threaten the manhood of the man of the house. This was the issue facing me in Nikhilgram today.

"*Assalamulaikum,*" I said. "May peace be with you." Taking a deep breath and pulling up the end of my sari to cover my head, I continued, "Your children were wonderful in showing me the way here from the bridge." I smiled, but nobody smiled back.

"Our wives will not make payments on their loans!" one of the men shouted at me. "What will you do about it?" I had been expecting a hostile reception, but this abrupt and aggressive start still took me aback. I looked at the crowd and then made direct eye contact with the man who had addressed me. My eye contact must have taken him by surprise, because he looked away nervously. Women in my culture are taught to show deference by looking at the ground and not looking directly into men's or elders' eyes when they speak. This custom is especially common in undereducated and underserved communities. It is as if the patriarchy must be reaffirmed constantly in case someone forgets it.

At that moment, I realized something. If I could challenge this hierarchy by simply looking a man in the eye, then that power structure rested on shaky ground.

"No payment. Ever!" the man repeated forcefully, but his voice quivered a little. His peers jumped in unison, nodding their heads in agreement. "Yes, yes. No payment, no payment!"

I noticed the women pulling their saris over their mouths. Looking closer, I realized that they were stifling giggles. In our social hierarchy, women are not allowed to speak over their husbands, so their reactions fascinated me. They knew their husbands were bluffing. And they knew the balance of power was shifting in their direction. The women's stifled laughter spoke clearly to their husbands. Go ahead and make a fool of yourself, but we all know what's going on here: I make more money than you now, you don't like it, and so now you are making a scene.

As I realized we were walking into a power dynamic shift rather than an actual inability to make loan repayments, I saw an opportunity. "*Bhaira*, brothers, I understand," I said, trying to sound kind but not condescending. "I am here to listen. Tell me: how bad is it now for you? Did you get a good crop before the rainy season started? How can we help you?"

The men's body language changed. Some squatted on the floor, and others simply relaxed their arms and jaws a bit. The men started talking, and I listened. They talked about how hard it is to make a living from such small plots of land. They appreciated the income from their wives' new businesses, but they wanted their wives to stop that work so they could help with the farm work. They believed the women would be better off helping them farm than running their own enterprises.

"Bhaira, from what it sounds like, the sisters here were helping, but it wasn't enough during the harvest," I summarized. "But now, during the rainy season, there's not that much farm work to do. How about you both work on the new business—which is your family's business—and make some money? Then, come autumn, sisters can focus more on the farm work and less on the new business. What do you think?"

Some men were nodding in agreement. After four hours of conversation and several rounds of hot tea—with milk from cows bought with Grameen loans—we came to an agreement. The men would work alongside the women in their businesses, and they would repay the loans starting next month, once the rainy season ended and the money pressure eased up a little. They also promised to start sending their children—including the girls—back to school. For me, getting the daughters back to school was at least as important, if not more, as the loan payment.

When we were about to leave, the women surrounded me. All of them were smiling through betel nut–stained teeth, and they showed their affection and gratitude in their own shy ways: stroking my arm and touching my face and head.

On the three-hour walk back to the Grameen office with my colleagues, I marveled at how weeks of rain had turned the paddy fields into lakes, which merged imperceptibly with the flowing river. Everywhere one looked was shimmering water. I took a deep breath, acknowledging that with this beauty came the hardship of village life. With hardship came ways of organizing family and social and economic life that disadvantaged women. And for one side to gain power, the other side had to accept the new power dynamic and give up a measure of their own.

Resistance to such rebalancing of power is almost assured, and working around that resistance would always be a challenge. Trying to keep my footing in the water that flowed all around us meant taking one careful, deliberate, defiant step at a time.

CHAPTER ELEVEN

When a Woman Signs Her Name

Brilliance and inventiveness do not come from expensive degrees but from passion and dire necessity. Sometimes when I was working on Wall Street, I'd look around at my colleagues and wonder if they were actually any smarter or harder working than some of the women who had raised me in Bangladesh. And now, working with Grameen Bank, I would often look at the women entrepreneurs and think: I could have easily been them. Sometimes I wondered what this or that woman could do if she had gotten the same education, opportunities, and connections the men I worked with at Morgan Stanley had received. I kept thinking about the sharp contrasts I had seen between the billions of dollars thrown around by Wall Street banks and the life-changing value of a single dollar for a woman in Bangladesh. These realizations made me even more determined to help these women.

One day, I visited a Grameen branch in Deujan, about forty kilometers from Shuruj Branch where I was living. I wanted to test a hypothesis I had developed about "borrower graduation." Every year, a successful borrower who repays her loan is offered a larger one. This is meant to help them expand their business, yet after a point, many entrepreneurs no longer know how to utilize the money. They don't know how to grow the business beyond a certain size, or they have difficulty accessing new markets to sell their product or service.

In some cases, they then find it difficult to repay their loans. In order to prevent defaults, I hypothesized, such borrowers should "graduate" from their microloan to a small enterprise loan and receive proper training in how to run a small business. My hypothesis had proven true in Shuruj, and I wanted to test it in Deujan.

Deujan is a weavers' area, part of the Tangail district famous for producing intricate saris. Almost every household has a loom. What an incredible amount of patience one needs to weave a sari. The designs are intricate and the threads fragile. The absolute attention to every detail required, for hour after hour of sitting at the loom, is immense. These women deserved to have their craft showcased to the world. Their talent, patience, creativity, and determination were unparalleled. My heart broke to see women defaulting on their loans for lack of access to a bigger market.

I wanted to visit a borrower who had successfully grown her business and turned it into a microenterprise. Rokeya greeted me at her house with a confident smile. I knew right away that she was a woman in charge of her life. The house was made of brick, and much sturdier than her neighbors' mud houses. She noticed me looking at the house and proudly informed me that she had built the house using a Grameen loan in her name. Then she offered to show me her small business. We walked to the back of the house to another, larger building, with low mud walls and a thatched roof. Ample sunlight streamed in and I saw four looms in use: one worked by a man and the other three by women. Her own loom, the fifth, was the only idle one.

I asked Rokeya how she had grown the business. Hers was the first microenterprise I had seen grow large enough to employ so many. I had assumed that Rokeya had no knowledge about business terminology like working capital or inventory, so I tried to explain my questions in simple terms. But she knew how to manage inventory, how to allocate raw materials, how to sell, and how to use working capital effectively. I was impressed, and I wondered whether perhaps Rokeya held the answer for how other women could grow their businesses and avoid defaulting as they got larger loans.

My hopes came crashing down, however, when I asked how much she paid her workers. Rokeya hemmed and hawed before finally answering, "Nothing."

"What? Nothing? How do you get away with that?" I asked.

Rokeya paused and then gave me the full story. "We are Muslim, and my husband can marry four women," she said. "So I told him to marry three more women. As you know, he needs the first wife's permission to marry again, and I gave my permission—with the condition that he and his new wives all work for me. Then, in return, I take care of them."

I was dumbfounded. I am rarely at a loss for words, but I truly did not know what to say. Rokeya saw my shock and continued in a hushed voice, confiding in me. It seemed important to her that I understand her decision-making process. "Apa, my husband worked the small plot his father passed down to him, but that barely fed us for a month!" she said matter-of-factly. "I had to feed him, my in-laws, and my two children. How could I do that? I know how to weave, but if I weave, I don't have time to take care of the household. I don't have time to take my saris to market and sell them. I got so tired of our money problems—not being able to grow my weaving business—and I was scared of not being able to pay my loan. And I was so tired of enduring my husband's constant complaints and beatings that I told him to marry again. This made him very happy. I taught him and his new wives how to weave, and now I support them with my business. Everyone is happy."

I looked at her and took her hand. "And you?" I asked her. "Are you happy?"

She looked straight into my eyes. "I am now able to take care of everyone and give my daughters an education," she said. "I can grow my business and have money of my own. I am now a free woman. Yes, that makes me happy."

Rokeya's story was sobering, and it was hardly a replicable model. But it showed me the lengths a determined entrepreneur would go to grow her business, especially when her children's future depends on it.

***

My days working with Grameen melted into one another as the slow rhythm of rural life took over. The routines of our work sometimes seemed mundane, but I never got bored by one thing: disbursing a woman's first loan.

Once a woman joined a Grameen group in her village, she was eligible for a loan. To receive a loan, the borrower, our new client, needed to come to the local Grameen Bank office and sign for the loan. She would then receive the money, along with a "passbook," which logged the loan disbursal and repayments.

Even in the 1990s, one out of five women in Bangladesh—and a much higher percentage in rural areas—could not read or write. That meant that they could not sign their loan documents. On most official documents, therefore, women "signed" using only their thumbprint. That blob of ink confirmed that the government systems did not care about their individual identity.

Grameen did not believe in thumbprint signatures. Instead, we promoted the powerful notion that each woman, like a real client, had to provide a written signature to receive a loan. So to sign for the first loan of their lives, women had to learn to sign their names.

Every morning outside our mud house of an office, women would stand in a line, waiting patiently to learn how to sign for their loans. As they waited, their heads covered with the end of their saris and eyes demurely downcast, these women would give us an occasional flash of eye contact. In that glance would shine a twinkle of excitement. They were so eager to learn to pull one of the levers of power available to them.

It's hard to capture in words the thrill of teaching a woman how to sign her name. Watching women take pride in their own names— names that now had legal bearing—brought deep joy. After bearing a child, most of these women were known in the village by their first child's name—Hasan-er Ma (Hasan's mother) or Fatimar Ma (Fatima's mother)—another practice that erased a woman's identity and power. But here at Grameen, they learned to sign their own name, the one their parents had given them.

"Hold the stick closer to the point," I coaxed a woman named Amina one morning. "I will hold your hand with mine, and we will practice writing your name in the dirt. Let's do it, Apa."

We crouched together on the ground and wrote "Amina" together in Bengali script. Amina was my age, but years of hardship, early childbirth, and an inadequate diet had taken their toll on her. She looked middle-aged. But today, the joy of a new beginning brought out the excited child inside her. Together, we wrote her name dozens of times, using a stick to draw on the mud. With each stroke, Amina seemed to get bolder and more confident.

"Apa, I can do it now. Can I practice on paper?"

Holding on tightly to the pen, Amina wrote her name on a piece of scrap paper until she got the hang of it. Then she was ready to sign on the official loan document.

I read aloud to her the terms of the loan. To make proper use of the loan and to abide by Grameen's social contract, she would agree to: send her children (both girls and boys) to school; plant vegetables around her house; build a pit latrine as soon as she could afford it; and neither give dowry for her daughters' marriages nor accept dowry for her sons'.

Then the moment came. With total concentration, Amina bent down to sign her name on the document. Knowing that this signature would transport her to a new life, she wrote a name that for the first time she was seeing in its own form, by her own hand. What may have looked like a first grader's penmanship to an outsider was the passionate accomplishment of a woman unleashing her own power.

Amina looked at me with tear-filled eyes. She took my hands in hers and touched them to her head.

As I wiped away my own tears, I handed her the money. "Amina, Apa, look at me," I said firmly. "Look. You are now a businesswoman. From now on, never look down when you speak to anyone. Others need to respect you. You are taking control of your life. And most importantly: you are my client now. Thank you for your business."

Though I repeated this ritual hundreds of times, I never got tired of it. No joy compares to helping someone find their dignity and showing them the source of their own power.

CHAPTER TWELVE

Build Your Own Bridge

Educated people from the Global South have a love-hate relationship with the almighty World Bank. The victors of World War II created the World Bank, along with the International Monetary Fund (IMF), to help newly independent countries get on their feet after centuries of colonial rule. The Bank, as it is known, focuses on infrastructure, social capital, and overall economic growth in developing economies. The IMF was established to focus on monetary and macroeconomic policy—helping the Philippines, for example, to adjust their foreign exchange reserves (dollars that they need to have in their coffers in order to import goods from other countries) and advising the government on the interest rates to keep the country's inflation in check. The Bank and the IMF worked closely in these efforts.

People from the former colonial powers—including the United States, which inherited several colonies via the Spanish-American War—still run the Bank. The World Bank president is always an American, and the Bank is headquartered in Washington, DC. The former colonial powers thought they knew what postcolonial countries needed, and most had good intentions. But the Bank staff weren't required to have any prior knowledge of the culture, norms, or history of a particular country before being assigned to "fix" it. This savior view of development was deeply embedded in the Bank at the time, as well as in the elite Western academic institutions that had trained its employees. Sadly, little has changed over the last seven decades of its existence.

I could feel this arrogance in the air as I walked into the headquarters of the World Bank in downtown Washington, DC. Two things had become clear toward the end of my time in Bangladesh: the recommendations I had proposed for Grameen Bank were unlikely to be implemented any time soon, and my parents' attempts to arrange a marriage for me were becoming too serious to laugh off. So I had returned to the United States to pursue graduate school and gotten a job as a research assistant in the East Africa Department of the Bank. I needed the money and was happy with the opportunity.

My salary was such a good amount of money—especially for an entry-level part-time professional staff—that I became curious to find out the salaries of all these people supposedly saving the world. What I found out surprised me. Not only were they paid very well; the list of perks—children's private education, interest-free housing loans, allowances for nonemployed spouses—far exceeded any I had ever seen at a private-sector employer. Now I understood why my classmates in graduate school were all vying for jobs at the Bank! Wall Street folks got a bad rap for being so interested in wealth, but at least they were upfront about their desire to earn money. Here I encountered a different kind of person: those who scoff at Wall Street and anything to do with the payoffs of a capitalist system while personally benefiting from very comfortable packages.

I had seen arrogance on Wall Street driven by the power of controlling financial markets, but the hubris around here was different. This arrogance grew from the power of controlling the day-to-day lives of billions of people across the globe through taking care of basic developmental needs: access to finance, livelihood, food, and necessary infrastructure.

Personal economic comfort contributed to staff's risk-averse behavior in the Bank. Nobody wanted to question the status quo if it could jeopardize their job in any way—even if that risk-taking could improve the lives of millions. This pattern became evident during conversations with my colleagues, some of whom understood very well the flaws of the systems they propagated.

"Durreen, the Bank is a massive ship," I heard frequently. "It's impossible to turn its course." The message was clear: this is how economic development has been practiced since the end of World War II. We have the blueprint; now follow it. The most you can do is make changes around the edges. But if the Bank was all-powerful, whose power did it work to preserve? Whom did it empower?

These contradictions confronted me in my very first assignment. My manager had tasked me with evaluating the nonperforming loans in the Bank's East Africa portfolio. "I'm happy to evaluate the loan performance from a financial angle, but I will be honest: I know nothing about any East African countries," I said. "I can learn, but I will need your help." How could I advise a government when I didn't yet know much about their country?

My manager and I sat together in his fancy office with plush chairs, an expansive view, and a small sitting area. What a far cry from the shared office rooms of Grameen, with their wooden desks and chairs, I thought. "You probably know a lot more than many people here," he said, leaning back. "At least you've spent time in the field with the underserved people whose lives we deal with. Most people here have no idea what life is like at the village level. Yes, they go for 'missions' now and then. But what can you learn about the people you are working for if you are staying in a fancy hotel in the capital city and taking Land Rovers for a quick visit to a Bank project? Not much. But that is how it is done at the Bank. I don't agree with it, but I put up with it because it allows me to be in the development field."

I liked my manager; he was smart and to the point in a gentle, polite way. Nevertheless, as he spoke, I couldn't help thinking that people make the choices they want to make. We often work within the constraints we set for ourselves. Why are we unable to imagine a different way of doing things?

Despite my misgivings, I was genuinely excited about working on this portfolio analysis. I wanted to use my skills and learn about a whole new continent. Frankly, I also wanted to find out what gave the

Bank so much power to shape fortunes around the world. On Wall Street, I had seen how the financial system recycles power within its own networks. At Grameen, I had watched women try to access that power. Now I wanted to figure out how international development fit into the equation. Was it a distributor of power or a protector of it?

***

The deeper I dug into the nonperforming loan portfolio, the more concerned I became. Why were *none* of these loans being paid off? There were reams of reports praising the loans as well as monitoring and evaluation studies of the projects that the Bank itself had produced. But why was there was no verification of all this positive impact by the people we were supposed to be serving? Where were *their* voices in evaluating the success of the projects? And why was there so little concern about the nonpayment of the loans?

I once again knocked on my manager's door to ask some questions. Engrossed in his work, he looked up and smiled, gesturing me to have a seat.

"It looks like none of the Bank loans are working," I said. "Not a single country is paying them off. Am I missing something here?"

"No, you are not missing anything," my manager said. "At this point, the entire East Africa portfolio is nonperforming, because in most cases the government is not making their part of the payment for the project."

"So the infrastructure and social projects are just half completed? The roads are half built? The bridges are half done? The schools are not functioning?" I asked incredulously. "Don't these countries need these projects to be successful in order for their economies to grow?" I couldn't believe what I was hearing.

"Your understanding is correct, Durreen, but various things may have happened," he answered. "For example, there may have been a government change, and the current government does not want to respect the previous government's plan. Or in some cases the government never wanted the project in the first place, but the folks at the Bank thought it was a good idea and pushed the loan on the country, possibly dangling some other carrot to have it approved."

My manager stood up and walked to the window. "So they got the loan approved, but now the country does not want to pay it. The officers who made the loans probably got a promotion for their 'great work' and are now in a different department here. They're not responsible for this nonperforming loan, which is on my plate now. Welcome to the Bank." He sounded bitter and resigned.

So this is how power is brokered by one of the most powerful organizations in the world, I thought: by reinforcing the status quo. Understanding and pursuing what the people of a particular country wanted seemed like not even an afterthought. This was so wrong. Where was the transparency? Where was the accountability?

I sat there in shock, probably a bit like a child who has just found out that Santa is not real. In that moment the magic disappears, but you still try to hold on to the hope of the illusion.

**

It was the end of May, and the vast veranda of the Carlyle House in Old Town Alexandria had become my paradise for the evening. There was still a slight chill in the air, but I was warm from the happiness of seeing my family and friends all gathered here for my wedding to Rob. The magnolia trees nestled up against the veranda were in full bloom, filling the air with their heady scent and engulfing us in the magic of the evening.

I had recently been accepted to Wharton Business School for a joint program with the Johns Hopkins School of Advanced International Studies (where I was currently studying) with a full scholarship. It would mean a move to Philadelphia. Rob's calm and immediate change of gears for his own career direction surprised me. "You should do the Wharton program," he said. "I'll transfer schools so we can be together. We can make it work." As I walked over to the gazebo with my parents on each side and saw him waiting with the imam, I felt a deep sense of clarity and peace.

The white-and-gold sari that Ma brought for me to wear, along with my grandmother's jewelry, made me, who usually hated to get dressed up, feel like a princess. At the reception I watched Rob dancing with my mother. Despite her love for social occasions, she had never danced before, but she seemed to be doing just fine. She was wearing a pink sari and beaming. I knew how relieved she was just to see me married, and a significant amount of family drama had preceded the wedding. To get to this point I'd had to defy so much. Whether it was my parents' desire for me to stay in Asia for university, expectations that I have an arranged marriage, or the belief of many that Wall Street was no place for a Bangladeshi woman: no matter which culture I lived in, I bumped up against the notion that we should stay on our own side of the bridge. The notion that we should simply accept our fate crosses cultures.

I was moved by how my mother had embraced Rob as her son-in-law, and it gave me hope that I could build and cross other bridges. Even Rob's parents, who rarely saw each other after their divorce, danced away to the lively jazz music. They really knew their moves, swinging and twirling.

I snapped out of daydreaming when Rob came over, tapping on his glass to make a toast. All the dancing, drinking, chatting, and music came to a hush. "Friends and family, thank you so very much for coming from all over the world to celebrate our wedding. Durreen and I are truly grateful. Now, please join me in a toast to the most beautiful and wonderful woman in this world, my bride—or, as they say in Bengali, my Bahu. To Bahu!" Rob said, raising his glass. "To Bahu!" chimed the crowd.

PART III

Connect the Haves and Have-Nots

CHAPTER THIRTEEN

Toward a Global Marketplace

"Bahu!" my friend Radhika called out from a distance. Central Park was bursting with flowers and kids running around when I found a bench under the shade of a tree to rest. I was supposed to meet Radhika here to catch up. And we had so much to catch up about.

Since our days at Smith, Radhika had become an embodiment of the Lower East Side. Free-spirited, creative, and optimistic, she was writing a book about how jazz musicians create music. Rob and I had been back in New York City for a few years: settling into our new careers, married life, falling right back into the intensity of the city with work and old friends. Rob had returned to investment banking and was now equipped with a law degree. He had found his groove doing billion-dollar merger and acquisition deals, helping giant companies join together or buy each other. He slipped right back into the intense routines of New York investment banking like they were a pair of old shoes.

Meanwhile, I had arrived at a dead end—several, in fact. My search to make finance do good for the 99 percent seemed imperiled. Graduate schools did not have the answers for me, nor did the bastion of development, the World Bank. Through my work experience and graduate school programs, I was creating a bridge between the vastly different domains of development and finance, but I felt so alone in making this connection.

I had interviewed with several community development banks in Philadelphia and the Greater New York area. While they were making capital available in a small way to small businesses in underserved communities, these banks were struggling. Their work was happening in a vacuum, without any connection to the larger financial markets and without access to capital to grow and lend to the community at larger scale.

Small and minority-owned businesses in underserved communities were hitting the same wall of selective bias. Even if they did receive capital from a bank—and that happened only with much difficulty—other operational challenges remained. These businesses tended to lack the "right" contacts, access to the "right" market, and sometimes simply the "right" strategy. In other words, a whole set of invisible business tools, beyond just money, enables small businesses to work—and when lacking, as in the case of many businesses owned by women and entrepreneurs of color, causes them to fail.

I observed micro- and small businesses in New York, Philadelphia, and Washington, DC, hitting a wall in their growth and potential positive impact in their community. Here in America, these businesses were bigger than those I had seen with Grameen, but there were a lot of similarities. Both types of businesses were located at the periphery of the financial system, without an entry to the inside. Both needed much more from the financial markets than they were getting. Making finance work for the underserved "takes a village," to crib a well-known phrase—but where was that village? Who was going to create it? Where was the pathway for these enterprises and the underserved communities they represent to financial markets that truly value their work?

Feeling disillusioned and unable to change a rigid system, I had left the financial sector for a job with Hearst, the multibillion-dollar media company. I was now overseeing the business of a dozen women's magazines. In my ever-evolving search to find the source of power and turn it inside-out, I had wandered into media, which I believed had incredible potential for public service by influencing hearts and minds. Media also had incredible power to influence public opinion and the financial market. It sat in the nexus of human development and economic opportunity with the power to unleash change. At least that is what I thought.

But now I had a fancy job at Hearst magazines, and I was feeling more disillusioned than ever. Could I really make a difference by informing women about twenty ways to get the man of their dreams or eight ways to make the perfect pie? I struggled to come to terms with what people wanted to read versus what was moral and just. Adding to the tension between consumer desire and what you think they *should* desire was the overarching pressure to create content that would attract the advertising dollar.

Even while our magazines were offering solutions for women to shape and control their bodies, I was feeling betrayed by mine. I was recovering from an ectopic pregnancy, which takes hold in the fallopian tube and can be fatal to the mother if not detected in time. Without knowing it, I had been six weeks pregnant when I started bleeding at work and fainted.

During the month of bed rest following my emergency surgery, I had spent time piecing together what had happened and how I felt about it. I had been *pregnant*? We certainly hadn't planned it. I had been traveling so much for my corporate job that I had lost track of many things in my life. I hadn't noticed anything different with my body other than chronic exhaustion. Now I had lost one fallopian tube, and my other tube had been severely damaged during my teenage years when my appendix ruptured. Sadness overwhelmed me.

Now I still tired easily, but I was healing. I was doing some work every day, trying my best to run a vast overseas media operation while sitting propped up on a bed, with a cordless landline phone, in a tiny New York apartment.

But it was hard to focus on the nuances of growing a magazine business on the other side of the world when my head was in a fog. I could not focus. Little made sense anymore. How strange it feels to mourn for something you did not even know you wanted.

***

Sitting on the park bench, I smiled as Radhika ran toward me with her big smile, crumpled linen shirt, and torn jeans. "Bahu!" she sang out again, her hair flowing behind her. She thought it was hilarious that Rob called me Bahu. "I mean, honestly, how cute and corny can it be?" she would laugh, and soon the teasing became a part of her vocabulary. So I was bride to Radhika now too.

Radhika engulfed me in a bear hug. "Bahu, how are you feeling? Are you OK?" she took my face in her hands. "You know it's OK, right? Being a mother does not define womanhood—screw what South Asian culture shoves down our throats. We are in America. Think of all that you have done here as a woman—and as a minority woman at that!"

I saw the love and concern in her shining eyes and started sobbing. "I am sorry," I said eventually, wiping my nose and resting my forehead on Radhika's shoulder. "I don't know why I am crying. I didn't think I wanted to have a baby. But now that I can't, I'm overwhelmed with sadness—and I'm angry! I'm angry with my body and my fate."

I thought I wanted to transform the world for inclusion and gender equality, I told Radhika, but I hadn't done anything. Yes, I could occasionally push through some meaningful content—like magazine covers featuring women of color or stories covering economic inequality. But so what? Did that move the needle at all? I felt full of despair, and my words showed it.

"Hey, this is not the Bahu I know!" Radhika said, pulling back to look me straight in the eye.

"The Bahu I know does not let anything pull her down. What happened to the new idea that was brewing?"

A few weeks earlier, I had told her my idea for a new company: one that would connect the haves and have-nots from across the globe, as producers and buyers on equal footing. I dreamed of an online global marketplace of handmade goods made by millions of women artisans, and small businesses. I had wondered aloud to her whether a marketplace would be the next stage of the microcredit movement. Not only would women have the chance to start small businesses making handmade goods, but they'd also have the opportunity to grow their business by accessing new markets through this new medium called the internet. A new online company for collectibles called eBay was getting people excited, I had mused to Radhika; surely the market would have an appetite for handmade gifts, household items, and fashion accessories from around the world.

"You're right," I told Radhika. "I need to put it down on paper and write a business plan." I smiled, feeling a nudge of something like hope in my stomach. "I mean, maybe this new global equalizer, the internet, can help me do it. It's 1999!" I said.

"Right!" Radhika said animatedly. "Now *this* is the Bahu I know!"

***

Writing a business plan is like taking the first step of a marathon—or maybe the first thousand steps. A business plan is basically a structured research paper in which you outline how you will create the business, who your customers will be, how you will grow, and what technology, marketing, and sales strategy you will need. The plan allows you to think through whether what you want to do is actually possible.

Once you ink the idea, having evaluated all the necessary parts of growth, you turn the ideas into numbers. The numbers tell you how much it will cost to make this idea a reality. It is the first reality check of an entrepreneur's journey, the stage during which the edge of idealism often collides with pragmatism. How will the revenue streams look? How much money do you need to get the company off the ground? Will you need outside funding and if so, where will you get it? You will not have all the answers yet as to whether your new venture will succeed or fail. But now you've got some structure to the thinking, a framework for the idea, and the numbers to back it up. Now you need to make the plan a reality.

My company, oneNest, would manifest my quest to connect the worlds of the haves and the have-nots. I wanted to empower women, artisans, and microbusinesses from underserved communities by connecting them with a global market to sell their goods. These goods would be handcrafted personal items and household goods—jewelry, shawls, scarves, photo frames, tablecloths, bedspreads—anything that you need in your day-to-day life and made with hands and from the heart from artisans all over the world. The market would improve not only their individual incomes but also the fate of their communities, mightily. We would give women access to a market to sell their products so that they could pay off the loans they had taken to expand their production, avoiding the fate of the Grameen borrowers who defaulted on their loans after a few years because they had no access to new markets to grow their business.

In my research for the business plan, I found that such a marketplace simply did not exist. The internet presented a perfect opportunity for bringing exquisite, fair-trade items, made by artisans around the world, together in one marketplace. Beautifully woven fabrics from Bangladesh, silk shawls from Cambodia, silver jewelry from Indonesia, glass-beaded purses from Kenya, ceramic bowls from Mexico: the oneNest platform would show photographs of these products and share the stories of how they were made and by whom, as well as the positive impact created by every purchase. By connecting the two worlds of the buyers and the sellers, we could move the needle on global income inequality.

Turning an idea into a plan and then into reality hinges on an entrepreneur's ability to convince friends, family, and acquaintances to contribute labor and funds. The two first believers in oneNest were Mohsin, a childhood friend of mine, and Vance, a friend from the corporate world. Both men believed in the power of the internet to democratize the market and connect the haves with the have-nots for sustainable growth. All three of us put in some seed money to pull together a prototype of the website.

We got to work right away. Mohsin pulled together the web developers, while Vance took care of operational aspects like logistics and delivery. My job as CEO was to design the platform, source the goods that would appeal to the Western market, ensure pricing and quality, attract the buyers, find the right partners for marketing, and start building the team and the business as a whole.

A market requires two sides to come together simultaneously: buyers and sellers. On one side, we built a list of artisans and small businesses making beautiful handmade products. Watching the first artisans post product listings on the website was thrilling. There was Usha from India, uploading pictures of her gorgeous blue-and-white block print cushion covers and bedspreads. Maria from Guatemala uploaded photos showcasing the thick silver jewelry that she made that honored Indigenous designs. Grace, an artisan from the Philippines, shared a touching story of how she and her daughter collected seashells from the beach next to her village to create small, delicate capiz bowls from mother of pearl. Each item had a heartwarming story of the creator's passion and purpose wrapped around it.

Even as listings from sellers began pouring in, we had to get their goods in front of direct consumers and small retail businesses. We started pulling together the buyers—mom-and-pop stores, gift companies, anyone and everyone who would buy artisanal gift items.

The technology had hiccups. In these early days of the internet, it was difficult to capture the beauty and exquisite artisanship of the handcrafted items. The photographs uploaded by vendors were often of poor quality and the descriptions inadequate. Sourcing and delivering the products, as well as enhancing their appearance on the website, were difficult tasks. Vance, Mohsin, and I were all working part-time from home, but we soon realized that arrangement was not sustainable. We needed to get an office, we needed to start working full time, and we needed to raise money to grow the business.

Even as the stress of our start-up began to build, I could feel an almost physical sense of satisfaction as the dots between my three domains—development, media, and finance—began connecting. I reached out to my contacts at various microfinance organizations, fair-trade organizations, and artisan groups around the world to get their members to list their products on oneNest. I reached out to my media friends to develop creative marketing channels for oneNest. My experience of running multiple offices across multiple time zones at Hearst was coming in handy as I engaged microbusinesses and media houses across multiple countries and faced hurdles of cross-border commerce.

We were ready to move into the next gear: figuring out how to harness the power of finance to help our embryonic business.

We needed funding.

CHAPTER FOURTEEN

Who Will Put the Equity in Equity?

Raising money is the single most stressful aspect of starting a business. You have a short period of time within which you need to find the right contacts, convince those people that your business is worth backing, address their fears about risk, persuade them of all the good that will come out of the business, promise them incredible returns, and finally convince them to write you a check.

To start, you need to have the right contacts to raise money (capital, as it is known in financial markets). Lack of contacts with investors kills many businesses at the inception stage—especially businesses founded by women and people of color, many of whom do not have inroads to the people who control the financial markets.

In theory, the success of fundraising should correlate to the brilliance and solidity of the business idea and plan. In reality, though, investors are investing in *you*, the person, as much as they are in your idea. Sadly, investment decisions are too often based on intangibles that incorporate implicit biases and invisible systemic barriers. Potential funders may not verbalize or even be aware of this, but they tend to trust entrepreneurs who look like them. If there is no incentive or obligation to do otherwise, people like to help people from their own tribes. These biases are concealed by a wonderfully flexible word in finance: risk. You as an entrepreneur can be deemed "risky" by investors—and thus not worth supporting—if you do not share their socioeconomic background, race, or gender.

If, instead of fundraising from investors, you want to borrow money from a bank, you need to put up collateral, such as your house or your car, to "derisk" the loan. Rob and I did not have any significant assets, so banks perceived a business loan of the size we needed to be too risky. This meant I would have to raise equity capital: I would have to convince potential shareholders to give money to the business in exchange for partial ownership. I needed to find people who would be comfortable with me, believe in me, and support my business.

I reached out to my friends and family to invite them to invest, and a few came through. Still, this was only a fraction of what was required to cover all the technology and operational costs to develop oneNest. We needed more.

The two most common questions potential financiers ask are: "Do you have skin in the game?" and "What traction does the business have?" They want to know that, as the entrepreneur, you are personally taking on the initial risk of the idea not working. In our case, all three of us had put in money to get the business off the ground, so we definitely had skin in the game. As for traction, you need a prototype—a smaller version of the business you ultimately want to build—so that you have physical evidence of your business model working. We had that as well.

As an entrepreneur seeking funding, you can't seem either too desperate or too confident. And you need a big dollop of luck. If only I had a Lakshmi—a good luck charm, like my mother for the small businesses in Dhaka. Well, my Lakshmi did appear when Rob mentioned oneNest to his colleagues at work and a group of them decided to invest. I was grateful for the capital that I could raise after a short series of presentations and meetings with Rob's high-finance colleagues. I knew they were investing more in Rob—the white man who was a lot like them—than they were in me, but I did not care. Lakshmi played her role, and I had my new investors.

So while we got our seed funding, also known as angel-round funding, I was filled with anxiety. What if I couldn't make oneNest work? What if I lost Rob's colleagues' money and it impacted his career? When these questions plagued me, I tried to stop my train of negative thinking by reversing its direction: What if oneNest did fabulously well and actually helped Rob's reputation?

Why do women so often think of what may go wrong instead of what may go *right*? Perhaps we have been so effectively conditioned by society to protect and preserve our loved ones and the status quo that we become risk averse. Embracing risk is an important element of being a successful entrepreneur or change-maker, and it's one that escapes a lot of women.

This was my first taste of the degree of risk you need to take as an entrepreneur. You convince people to believe in you—and then you need to make sure that you don't let them down. This weight of other people's expectations is an incredible burden to carry.

Yet deep down, I believed oneNest was a burden worth taking on, because I believed in the work that we were doing. I knew that if we were successful, then the lives of hundreds of thousands of people living in poverty across the globe would improve. By connecting artisans from underserved communities to markets they could not otherwise access, we were creating a new way of doing business. We were linking markets that had never been connected before.

In many ways we were not only creating a company; we were also creating a whole new industry. That required a whole new infrastructure. Connecting the internet to small sellers all over the world was a mammoth undertaking; I just didn't realize how mammoth.

***

So we needed money to create both a company and an industry at the same time. After investing all of the money from the angel-round investors in building our new marketplace, we still needed more money to scale our customer base and push the business forward. We needed to move to the next stage: raising capital from venture capital funds (VCs). VCs raise money from wealthy individuals and institutions and promise to generate a return by investing that money directly into newly formed companies like oneNest. VCs hold the key to the next round of funding required by a growth-stage company: one that is no longer just an idea or a small business but that is ready for the next stage of expansive growth.

Try as I might, I couldn't get any doors to open in the VC firms on the East Coast. I sent email after email and made phone call after phone call to the VCs in Boston and New York, but I could not get beyond the lowest-level employee. In the few meetings that I did manage to get with a midlevel staff person, through Wharton contacts or friends from Wall Street, the message was clear: nobody cared about business doing good. Creating a global marketplace for artisan goods? Too risky. The bottom line: there was no potential for growth for an online marketplace for products other than books or collectibles.

I began reading, with much envy, that more than 40 percent of all venture capital funding in the United States was going into internet companies. If entities with feeble business models of selling pet products, children's toys, and government forms could raise millions of dollars, why couldn't I? Nobody asked if these male founders actually knew how to run a business or if the company was meeting an essential market demand. The exuberance for internet companies continued, with the financial markets throwing money at these companies in a race to get bigger, faster. Companies without any proprietary technology or unique business model were spending a fortune on marketing to establish a brand that would give them the edge—an edge that they simply had not earned.

What was making the VCs support the companies they were supporting? After doing some research, I came up with three answers. First, venture capital firms were supporting companies that were taking an existing brick-and-mortar business online, whether it made sense or not. Second, all the businesses receiving funding were very US-focused, doing business primarily within our borders. And third and most important: the founders of companies receiving venture capital were all from the same demographic as the VC funders: white, a few Asians, and all men.

I wish I could say things have changed, but sadly, this third trend is still in place two decades later. Studies show that less than 2.8 percent of all VC funds go to women entrepreneurs. And even this low number is in sharp decline; the COVID-19 pandemic has led VCs to adopt even more "pattern-matching" habits, meaning investing in companies (and entrepreneurs) that are similar to the companies and entrepreneurs already in their portfolios. Women represent fewer than 12 percent of the management of VC funds. In terms of capital flow, women of color continue to receive less than half a percent of the total funds raised by new ventures.

OK, I thought, so I am a woman from Bangladesh who does not have buddies in the VC community. But our company held a key to make thousands of people's lives better and to create a lot of financial value for all the stakeholders involved. These facts alone meant I would not give up until I got to the money.

***

"Hello, is this Mr. Steiner? Mr. Steiner, this is Durreen Shahnaz. You may remember that we met at the VC conference in New York?" I took a deep breath, clutched the phone tighter, and kept going. "You said you liked my business and asked me to reach out to you if I was ever in Silicon Valley. Well, I am coming to town next week, and I was wondering if you would be interested in meeting with me?" Biting my lip as I waited for his response, I hoped that Mr. Steiner did not call my bluff.

The truth was that I had never met Mr. Steiner—nor any of the top people in the top VC firms I cold-called. Yes, I lied. I had never met any of these people. Did I feel terrible about my untruth? Yes, absolutely. Did I have any other way of getting to them? No.

So here I was, an entrepreneur with a cool technology solution for a global marketplace. I had more than proof of concept; I had actual traction in the market. I was already connecting thousands of buyers with sellers. In addition, I had the experience of running businesses, and I had also managed to pull an angel round of investment together. I knew oneNest deserved to be funded and that the future of talented but impoverished producers depended on my ability to get a venture capitalist on board with our vision. I just needed to get a few minutes in front of these people.

I talked myself into eight meetings. Vance, my cofounder, and I took a red-eye to San Francisco to save on one night's hotel fare. After eating breakfast and freshening up at a deli, I felt ready to take on Silicon Valley. Recharged and refreshed, we jumped back in our rental car and drove to the first meeting. We had eight meetings over the next eight hours.

I walked into the first meeting, and then the next, and the next, and they were all the same. I would walk into the room with full confidence in my accomplishments and the merits of our business. The venture capital firm representatives in every room were white men, with a smattering of Indian and Chinese men. As we entered each conference room, they would walk over to Vance and hold out their hands to shake his, assuming he was the CEO. I'd step forward and introduce myself as the CEO.

You might think that, upon realizing their mistake, the men would have been embarrassed or apologetic or at least confused. Instead, most of the time I just received a look of amused arrogance. A couple of the venture capital guys even said to Vance, "Hey, why aren't *you* the CEO?"

As meeting after meeting unfolded, we began to feel like someone had just kept pushing "replay" on a bad movie. It was apparent that people in Silicon Valley would invest only in people who looked like them.

In situations like this, you've got two options: accept the position people put you in or let your defiance kick in. The first option is tempting, especially when you're exhausted. But defiant optimism means sticking to your belief that your work is important. It means banging on door after door until one opens. And I kept reminding myself that I was banging on doors not only for myself but for the thousands of small business owners, women entrepreneurs, and families I was representing. We were bringing them to markets they could not be a part of otherwise. We had to keep going.

CHAPTER FIFTEEN

A Growth Mindset

One year into the business, after putting out countless fires and celebrating a few important victories, I realized how many factors lay beyond our control.

We had moved our young company into an office in downtown New York City, in an area called Hanover Square, just a few blocks from the World Trade Center. The rent was affordable because the buildings in this corner of the financial district were from the turn of the nineteenth century. They were grand and ornate but antiquated buildings, hugging the narrow roads feeding into Wall Street. Our floor of the building had high ceilings and an open-office layout. Vance, Mohsin, and I were on a creative high as we grew the business piece by piece: adding technology upgrades, finding ways to get more businesses to sign up on the platform, nurturing smaller customers, and starting to think about bigger buyers.

My mantra was the so-called 80-20 rule: we needed 20 percent of the buyers to be responsible for 80 percent of the sales. Otherwise, it would be too much work to manage so many buyers. This meant we needed to focus on business-to-business, or B2B, sales: sales to big catalog companies and department stores.

We created oneNest to connect impact to products, focusing on the maker of the products and her life. We shared stories from Fatema in Bangladesh, who used vegetable dyes to color the yarn for silk shawls; from Mei in Cambodia, who continued the family tradition of making silver bowls with intricate traditional Angkor designs; and from Adjua in Ghana, who trained village youth to create traditional mud cloth. We loved helping artisans continue great local traditions by directly enabling them to sell their products and support their families and communities. We believed these stories of direct impact would make our customers value the products more. Certainly, our buyers would be eager to support these global women's livelihoods.

We were wrong. Our customers, both individuals and stores, cared more about price than all other factors. Price always came before the cause. We found ourselves scrambling to bring down costs while still retaining customers and offering the makers a fair price for their work.

We also realized that once they ordered, our buyers did not want to wait to receive products. To speed up delivery, we had to preorder products that we forecasted would sell more and keep them in storage as inventory on hand. Managing inventory is a complex science, so we entered into a partnership with a company that would do it for us. We started getting some large orders, which was exciting, but our artisans could not produce the number of goods our buyers wanted without receiving working capital upfront. So soon we found ourselves doing trade financing, which means giving upfront money to the producers to make the products *before* we got paid by the buyers.

The complexity of the business kept growing from every direction. We were now managing inventory, pricing, and financing for small businesses across the globe. In a business start-up, just when you feel like you have solved one problem, ten new hurdles pop up. You have to remind yourself that it is a marathon, not a sprint. But as I sat with the numbers, they were telling me I did not have enough fuel for a marathon. We were burning through money more quickly than we were making it. I was determined to make ends meet both by increasing revenue and by finding funders.

My determination was intensifying in another realm of life too, as I made the decision to begin IVF treatment to try to conceive. I needed to control something in my life, so if it was not going to be the VCs, then it was going to be my reproductive system. This was not very rational thinking, but sometimes you need to fuel the heart to move forward. Just as my head ached to find a solution to raise capital for oneNest, my heart ached to hold a baby.

So after a long day at work, I would go home to an empty apartment, as Rob would usually still be at work. I would take out the syringe, jab it into the bottle, and then muster up the courage to inject it into my belly and the side of my hip. It is shockingly difficult to inject oneself. You hold up a portion of the flesh with the thumb and forefinger of one hand and prick the needle and push down the syringe handle with the other hand. Then you feel the thick liquid seeping and pain traveling through your body.

As tears pricked my eyes, I had to keep telling myself that this was the price of creating something. Raising a company and having a baby: I knew my tears were related to both. These longings gave shape to everything, and at times both seemed like impossibilities.

***

Despite the challenges, oneNest kept on growing. Our product listings grew from dozens to hundreds to a few thousand units. Handmade wonders from around the world were finding eager buyers. The mom-and-pop stores were buying at a steady pace and coming back for larger orders. Catalog companies and department stores were starting to put in bulk orders. Our mission to create a more egalitarian world through a marketplace created a halo of goodwill that kept us going.

We also managed to get some VC funding from very unusual sources, including a Middle Eastern fund and a new women-focused fund. Finally, there was enough funding to push ahead with our work.

As our network grew, our vision came to life, especially when we helped communities rebuild through our work. One such call to action came when a devastating earthquake hit Gujarat, India, in January 2001. The earthquake registered 7.7 on the Richter scale;

in 110 seconds it destroyed buildings, houses, and roads. The earthquake wiped out several villages, killed close to 20,000 people, and injured more than 160,000. It reminded me of the devastating cyclone in Bangladesh and how my bank colleagues had rallied around a fundraising effort. The need was similar, but this time I longed to focus on building long-term resilience. Survivors were receiving immediate relief from other organizations and efforts; but how could we play a role in sustaining a village after the initial outpouring of charity dried up?

Through one of our partners, we connected a village of weavers with the initial capital to make silk shawls, which oneNest then sold through UNICEF catalogs in Japan. The initiative brought half a million dollars of income to the weavers in the devastated area, which helped them rebuild their village. We had helped an entire community determine their own destiny in the wake of disaster, in contrast to depending on foreign aid or handouts.

Although we had no money for marketing, word started spreading about oneNest's work, and we received an outpouring of requests from artisan groups around the world. Could we help them reach new markets? One such request came from Negros Occidental, one of the poorest islands of the Philippines. I'll never forget the day I opened a package with a note inside that read: "We are writing to you from a microfinance organization called Negros Women for Tomorrow Fund. We give small loans to women to run businesses. However, due to the recent global downturn in the market for sugar, which is a dominant crop on our island, we are now faced with a devastating economy and famine. Can you please help us sell the handicrafts our women borrowers make?"

My heart broke as I read the note, and I knew the answer: "Yes!" This had been my vision all along: to bring together the haves with the have-nots on equal footing, finding a place that would enable each to benefit from the other. I wanted to make every disadvantaged person in this world part of a greater economic system. I wanted to create a system that embraced and included, and that screamed to the world, "You can't ignore us!" I wanted to honor the defiant hopes of women like those from Negros Occidental, of women everywhere: to feed themselves and their families, to educate their children, and to make beautiful things that last.

***

Coming home to New York from a long business trip, I felt sick to my stomach. As soon as the taxi reached home from the airport, I left my bags with Rob at the steps of the brownstone on the Upper West Side in which we rented an apartment and headed straight to the neighborhood drugstore. I grabbed a couple of pregnancy kits, paid for them, and ran back to the house. Rob had taken my duffle bag upstairs already. I ran up the four flights of stairs, jumping two steps at a time, pushed open the door, and ran for the bathroom.

"Are you OK?" Rob said, concerned, through the door.

I opened the first kit, put it through the test, and held the stick with a shaking hand. One pink line became visible. I held my breath. I had been here before.

"Please, please, please let the second line appear . . . " I had my eyes squeezed shut, trying to will the second line to magically appear. When I opened my eyes and looked down at the stick, I saw the second line.

I couldn't believe it, and I kept on shaking my head. I had to be doubly sure. I opened the second kit and did another test. Again, two lines.

I gingerly opened the door. Rob was waiting, looking worried.

"Are you OK?" He repeated.

I smiled and nodded. I held out the stick for him to see.

"We did it!" I told him through tears. "We are having a baby! I know this one will stay with us. I can feel it. She will be a special one." I rested my head on his chest, held him tight as he pulled me closer and kissed the top of my head.

That day several years earlier, on the park bench with Radhika, I had felt so very far from who I was, what I was meant to be doing. I had felt like a train rolling off the tracks, straying far from my own direction and even questioning the direction I needed to go. Today, at last, I felt my life was on track, living and knowing my purpose once again. Whether it was a company, a child, or a vision for a more equitable world, I longed to bring vessels of hope to life. No matter what form they took, I would nurture them, and give my heart and soul to help them grow.

CHAPTER SIXTEEN

The Day Papers Fell from the Sky

Five months pregnant, wearing black maternity pants and a roomy white blouse, I was running late for a meeting at the oneNest office downtown. On my feet, I wore a pair of red Mary Janes.

While Rob and our families were thrilled about my pregnancy, our investors had not welcomed the news. They were furious. They had used words like "irresponsible," "unreliable," and "undependable." I assured my investors that I would not drop the ball and would continue with all my duties as a CEO no matter what. My pregnancy did not diminish my dedication as an entrepreneur. I wouldn't let them down.

As I continued the grueling hours of work to prove my invincibility, however, my body was starting to feel heavy. Were the investors right about me not being able to handle pregnancy and then motherhood while running a company? I knew it was silly, but I felt like I needed the magic from a pair of red shoes to give me the extra bounce of hope, just like my red shoes had during the war three decades ago.

Climbing the stairs from the Wall Street subway platform to the street, I saw them: hundreds of pieces of paper, floating down from the clear blue sky like huge snowflakes. At first I thought the papers might be coupons for free slices of pizza or reduced-rate haircuts. But as I picked a few up from the sidewalk, I saw the papers were memoranda and legal briefs and business analyses. Business documents lay everywhere on the sidewalk now. It was as if dozens of overstuffed file cabinets had vomited their contents onto the streets of Lower Manhattan.

I dropped the papers back to the sidewalk in shock and slowly turned my attention to the people standing around me. They were looking up. Craning my head, I spied a plume of smoke extending from one of the buildings of the World Trade Center.

"What happened?" I asked breathlessly.

"It was a plane," a man in a suit with a crooked tie said. My mind snapped to that other plane—the fireball crashing into my backyard all those years ago. Three decades later, here I was, witnessing the aftermath of another plane crash.

"Probably some rich guy who thought he knew how to fly a plane," the man answered, shaking his head. "That, or one of those damned sightseeing planes flying too low."

Those poor people, I thought. Had any survived? Had they sought cover? Was help coming for those who were fleeing and needed a way out? As the whole world would soon discover, something far bigger—far more frightening—than we could imagine was at work. I quickly walked to our office, just blocks from the World Trade Center, uneasy but still unaware of what was unfolding.

Reaching my office on the thirteenth floor, my heart racing, I sat down behind my desk. Like so many in the vicinity that day, I thought the situation at the World Trade Center was a bizarre accident. Vance and I instructed our colleagues who had arrived to start calling the staff who were not there yet and ask them to stay home.

As we began to make calls, I received an email from my father in Bangladesh. "Two commercial planes flew into the Twin Towers, just blocks from you. Are you OK? We're watching this live on television. We can't get through to you on the phone."

What was happening? I picked up the phone: no dial tone.

My anxious colleagues were huddling and speaking in low voices, throwing furtive glances at me. The safety of the group was my responsibility. A couple of them told me that they were leaving, but I was more scared about the unknown outside than I was of staying inside the building. "Don't go. We'll be safe in here," I said, with more clarity and confidence than I felt.

Just as I said that, the power went out. There we were, on the thirteenth floor of a building just a few blocks from what was now a massive disaster scene, sitting in the dark. And then came that other feeling—a tightness in my chest I hadn't experienced since my childhood, when I used to get bad asthma attacks. My breath was getting more labored.

I was walking over to my desk to get my inhaler when a massive sound ripped the air, like the bombs I often heard in my childhood. Somehow, I knew immediately that one of the towers had collapsed. Soot filled the air, and the electric blue sky outside suddenly turned to a dark gray, almost black, as if someone had pulled a thick blanket over our heads. I felt that fight-or-flight feeling that takes hold deep in the pit of your stomach and then spreads to your chest and the back of your throat. Equal parts terror and incredulity, that feeling caused my heart to pound and my brain to race: Is this it? Is this how it ends?

I took another puff from my inhaler and shouted to my colleagues to go through everyone's gym bags and pull out the T-shirts. The room was filling up with a strange acidic smell, and soot and smoke were seeping through the window cracks. I filled the bathroom sinks with water and soaked the T-shirts and towels as my colleagues brought them over. We stuffed the wet T-shirts around the windows and doors to stop the smoke and soot from coming in. But it wasn't working. We were engulfed in the black cloud.

"Cover your nose and mouth with the wet cloth," I barked. "Don't inhale the smoke. Sit on the floor, because the air may be a little better closer to the floor." Trying to remember the basic rules of saving oneself from smoke inhalation, I could feel my asthma getting worse and my lungs constricting. It will all be OK, I told myself over and over again. We will all live, I thought, my thoughts turning into prayers. *Please let everyone live.*

I decided it was no longer safe for us to stay. Somehow we needed to get down from the thirteenth floor and outside; otherwise we'd be trapped. So we gathered a few things and walked out of our office. Hurrying past the elevator, we saw no lights blinking on top of the elevator doors. Of course, with no electricity, the elevators were out as well. The only way out was to take thirteen flights of stairs.

Reaching the stairwell, we joined hundreds of other people hurrying to safety. The stairs were narrow, pitch black, and filled with smoke and soot. The pushing and shoving were frightening, and I could not move fast in my pregnant and asthmatic state. Vance took my hand to make sure that I did not fall. He and I both knew if I fell, I wouldn't be able to get up again. It was a stampede, and I needed to somehow keep up the pace in the dark, with very little oxygen going through my body.

Yet the trek down the stairs was not the most jarring part of the experience, nor was the black smoke that awaited us when we finally made it out of the building. Not even the surreal scenes that would greet us as we joined the throngs of people in the streets, stumbling toward safety, quite matched the fear I would face in the lobby.

***

I'd seen him on the elevator countless times. He was a middle-aged white man and usually wore a nondescript suit with a nondescript tie. He worked on another floor of our office building, and I recognized him as he walked toward my colleagues and me. We were huddled in the lobby, trying to decide whether to stay there in our building or to make our way out into the rubble and the smoke to find our way back to our families.

I saw him out of the corner of my eye as he approached our little group. His eyes were animated by a fury that was terrifying, and his glare was directed straight at me. "Two planes crashed into the World Trade Center, and it was done by fucking Muslims," he hissed. "I will kill *all* the Muslims!"

My heart raced, and I clung to my stomach. I had been so relieved to reach the first-floor lobby, thinking we were finally in a relatively safe place. But now it felt like the vortex of a spinning circle of danger.

"Are *you* a fucking Muslim?" he demanded, glaring down at me and breathing heavily. His body seemed to exhale hatred. Standing there in the darkened lobby, my white blouse stained by sweat and soot, I blinked back tears of disbelief. It was clear to me that the man's threats weren't the random ranting of a frightened man, speaking to no one in particular. This man, with whom I'd shared many elevator rides on the way to work, was speaking straight to me. These were the words of a man who hated me because of my skin color.

I said nothing. I needed to survive, and so I started walking toward the door. At this moment it was safer for me outside in the streets, where it felt like downtown Manhattan was being obliterated, than it was inside.

My colleagues joined me as I pushed my way out of the crowd in the lobby. The heavy glass doors opened into a fog of soot. We could barely see anything in front of us, and we were still holding wet T-shirts to our mouths and noses in order to breathe. We walked slowly, one step in front of another. Streams of people were walking away from what would become known as Ground Zero, and we joined them. Covered in ashes of death, some of us were hurt and bleeding, some were howling in pain, and some were collapsing on the street or sidewalk. Most of us were just numb, walking away from the flames of death toward what we hoped was survival.

After a few blocks, I braced myself and looked back. It was a horrific, surreal landscape, enclosed by mountains of fire, rubble, and destruction. I closed my eyes to say a prayer for all those who did not make it. We turned back and kept walking, dragging one foot in front of another. My red Mary Janes were now as black as the rest of my body. We pushed on.

As we came close to the East Village, the air began to clear. People were already setting up makeshift first-aid tables and handing out water bottles. "Please let us help you. You are pregnant. Sit for a moment," I heard someone say to me. The kindness barely registered, and I just shook my head. I needed to keep walking. We split up as a group, walking toward different destinations. Vance kept walking with me and repeating to himself and to me, "It is OK. We made it out. The baby will be OK. We will be OK." I did not say anything. I just kept walking toward the sunshine, which I could now make out in the distance filtering through smoke-filled air.

Ninety blocks and five hours later, I found my way to Isa's apartment, where Rob was waiting and living his own nightmare, as he thought I had died. As Rob opened the door, I collapsed in his arms, and he held me tight.

I closed my eyes and buried my face into Rob's white shirt. A sense of relief washed over me, but only for a moment. "Are *you* a fucking Muslim?" still echoed in my ears.

***

A few days later, I gathered enough energy to visit a makeshift memorial for the heroes of 9/11 in Union Square. I walked slowly from the subway to the memorial, taking in the graffiti on the walls of buildings: "Muslim Pigs." "Kill the fucking Moslems!" Was this the same America I had lived in just a week ago?

Taking deep breaths, I joined the line of people laying flowers at the memorial. I still felt raw, but I needed to pay respects to the ones who had died. I had read in the papers about the many ordinary people who like me had just arrived at work on a sunny September morning. I thought of the people in the subway with me that morning. How many of them made it out alive that day? Which of their lives were brutally ended? I thought of the first responders, the police officers, and the firefighters who ran into the buildings, toward the emergency, as everyone else was trying to escape. I thought of the young woman who interviewed for a job with our company but who had ended up accepting an offer at one of the offices high up in the Twin Towers. If I could have talked her into working with us, maybe she would be alive today. Almost three thousand lives were gone in a blink of an eye. Why wasn't I one of them? Why did I live? I was overwhelmed with survivor's guilt as I came to the front of the line.

I was getting ready to put my flowers down in front of the memorial when the man beside me looked straight at me and asked, "Are you a Muslim?"

I was taken by surprise and looked at him blankly.

"You are, aren't you?" he said. "We don't want your goddamn flowers. Go back to your fucking country!" Then he spat at me loud enough for everyone around to hear it.

For a moment I saw the other man's face in my mind too—the one from the smoke-filled lobby on that awful day. Now, however, instead of fear, rage rose inside me. Everyone was watching us now. I turned toward him and looked him in the eye.

"I am a 9/11 survivor, and yes, I am a Muslim and an American," I said evenly. "I am here to pay my respects and to prove to the people who did this that they cannot destroy the resilience of a New Yorker, no matter how much they try. We all need to rebuild the city together and honor the people who gave their lives for our city."

I found myself touching my belly, reassuring my baby that this would be her city too—that I was fighting for our city and our people. People around us broke into applause as I nodded at the man and walked away.

Two plane crashes have altered the course of my life. In a strange way, those plane crashes prompted me to begin connecting what happens on the back streets of the world to the power of Wall Street. They are responsible, in some way, for instilling in me the courage to connect those streets no matter what.

One plane crash—the one in my backyard during the war—put me on the path to leave home. It prompted me to seek a new life, free of war and rife with opportunity. Now, in an instant, another crash was beginning to pull me back to those roots I had fled. This one was now pulling me down the path I was meant to walk. One crash had shown me all that could go wrong with the world. The other was reminding me of the urgency to look for what was right.

CHAPTER SEVENTEEN

Things Fall Apart

The air in Lower Manhattan was still thick with fog when Diya was born. The cleanup of Ground Zero continued, but the mountain of rubble continued to smolder. A gray cloud filled with debris hung over Lower Manhattan. It was a fog that wouldn't lift.

But Diya, that lovely little bundle of joy, was a light shining through that cloud of dust for us. She was born on January 2, 2002, with Rob at my side. From the beginning she was a New Yorker. She was cuddly and happy, with a little tuft of soft brown hair and a great sense of independence. I'd wondered for so long when, or if, I'd ever become a mother. And now at last I had my answer.

Diya was hope personified. Diya's name meant light in several languages. Diya brought light to our lives in our dark city. And now, I was determined, more than ever, to make the world she'd entered a better place so that her light could shine through.

I returned to my post as CEO at oneNest a few days after Diya's birth. I was in charge of a company, and I had promised the investors that my maternal status would not change my commitment to the company or my performance as CEO. And so, my breasts heavy with milk, a breast pump in my purse, and large bandages on the incision in my lower abdomen, I returned to work.

As a working mother, I was constantly juggling expectations: running a company; keeping customers, employees, and investors happy;

keeping a household and marriage going; keeping in touch with my family; and now raising a baby. Thankfully, we had found a woman to help out with Diya's care. Indira had never been employed before, but she had raised four children in India and the United States, and that was good enough for me. I needed a mother to understand another mother.

The challenges with investors continued. Alan Greenspan, chair of the Federal Reserve Bank, had put an end to what he called the "irrational exuberance" of the dot-com bubble by increasing interest rates. This signaled an end to easy capital, market overconfidence, and, frankly, pure speculation. The dot-com companies that in initial public offerings had seen their stock prices triple in one day, now sat on stocks that were rapidly becoming worthless. These overvalued companies started folding, and trillions of dollars of investment capital simply evaporated. It all felt like a bad game of poker: a market exuberance that had been based on who you could fool. As with any bubble, during this era a handful of people—the 1 percent—became richer at the expense of the rest of the economy.

In the months that followed 9/11, as we crossed police barriers to reach the office that had been shut for weeks, I thought that all we needed was more time for word of oneNest to spread. Once the marketing takes hold, I believed, the company would grow more quickly. Instead, the world economy went into shock after 9/11. Nobody knew what would happen, so everyone became risk averse. Our sales numbers started declining, and the strain of maintaining operations while being surrounded by Ground Zero started taking a toll on my team.

By the fall of 2002, Diya was learning to crawl (backward), and the VC investors in oneNest were making their views clear. It would be best for the company's growth trajectory if we pivoted toward a brick-and-mortar approach. This would allow us to take on bigger customers and have larger B2B sales, which, in turn, would get the company closer and quicker to an "exit"—a trade sale. In other words, they wanted us to prepare to sell oneNest to another company. They wanted more growth, and they wanted it faster, so that they would get a bigger financial value for the company and their investment.

When you raise capital for your company by selling shares in your company, known as "raising equity," on one hand, it is a relief; you receive funding that you don't have to pay back the way you would a loan. On the other hand, you have new owners in the company—owners who have their own ideas about how it should evolve. Depending on how desperate you are for capital, you as the entrepreneur may end up giving up a lot of power over the direction of the company.

By this point in oneNest's journey, investors owned most of the company, and they were calling the shots. The pressure to grow even more rapidly started taking a toll on the team. The three of us who had started the company had all been working for very low salaries since we started oneNest. Mohsin told me he had decided to leave the company; he could not keep up with the pace, and he needed to draw a larger salary to support his family. When I looked to lean on Vance, he informed me that he, too, was going through a variety of personal and financial issues and that he had to leave as well.

I frequently fought back tears and put up a brave face in front of the staff. I was on my own now, and I agonized about how to spin this to the investors so that they didn't completely lose faith in me. I could not quit on the rest of the team, the investors, and especially the women who relied on oneNest to connect them to customers. When you remember how many people are depending on you, your options narrow.

When I announced Vance's departure to the team, they were disappointed and shocked. I put up a brave face and tried to rally them with visions of the good things yet to come. As an entrepreneur and CEO, I was constantly selling: selling an idea, a vision, and a promise to the team and investors. I smiled, I cheered, and I reassured, even while inside I was crying. I kept on telling myself: You can do this. You *have* to do this. You have no choice. Too many people are counting on you; oneNest is your child, a mother never quits on her child.

The investors were not happy with all these changes in the company, and they started their own planning. Perhaps these senior management departures are a sign that the company is not going in the right direction, they told me. The investors' solution? A "new face" for the company. It was time, they suggested, for me to step aside. My services as CEO were no longer needed.

I was humiliated but not surprised. While launching the company, I'd seen how quickly many potential investors had dismissed a brown woman. Whenever I entered the room with a male colleague—even if the man knew less than I did and had a less senior role—all eyes and ears were directed toward him instead of me. Now I was not only a minority woman but also a mother—in their eyes, a double liability. After Diya's birth, my loyalty to the company I had founded was continually questioned. It felt like others were making the choice for me, telling me that I couldn't have it all. I could try with all my might to fight discrimination, but it was difficult for me to overcome the reality that business in 2002 remained a man's world—and a white man's world at that.

I was worried for the future of oneNest, and for the thousands of small businesses all over the world that depended on the growth of our company. I was worried for the fate of the new market infrastructure we were creating for equitable economic development. But I had little choice other than to go along with the investors' wishes. And so while the investors made plans to introduce a new CEO to the company, I assumed the role of oneNest's chairperson, charged with the task of bringing in capital for oneNest's growth or, if need be, looking for a buyer for the company.

The new CEO handpicked by the investors to be my successor was everything they thought they wanted. He was a white man who came from a major retail catalog company in corporate America. He was familiar with the inner workings of brick-and-mortar retail institutions, which was the business model our investors wanted oneNest to embrace.

And just like that—one year after two planes hit the World Trade Center and a few short months after becoming a mother—I found myself passing the reins of the company I'd dreamed up, nurtured, and cultivated to someone else.

***

The air was cold and crisp during those fall and winter months. By day, I worked to find a buyer and to keep things moving forward at oneNest. By night, I came home to little Diya. I'd arrive home around 6:00 p.m. and, after donning my workout clothes, help Indira place Diya in her jogging stroller beneath layers of warm blankets and a plastic wind cover.

Then I would run toward the southern tip of Manhattan, to Battery Park, pushing Diya along, Lady Liberty coming into view on our right halfway through the run. As I ran, I would reflect on the long day and the year of loss.

It's a strange thing, working to sell a company you've built before it has realized its potential. There's a lot of wondering and wishing. When you're an entrepreneur, you jump in to solve a market problem. You create a solution, but you do not have sole control over the growth of the company. It takes time for the market to embrace the solution, but when it does, you know you are on the right track and your sales figures start reflecting that. We had proven that there was a market problem: thousands of small businesses in underserved communities and women entrepreneurs without access to a market for their products. I knew oneNest had its hiccups, but I didn't think now was the time to sell it.

As a new mother, I saw a lot of parallels between Diya's growth and the company's. Like a mother, an entrepreneur gives birth to a company and knows when the company is ready to crawl, walk, and run. Despite a rough start, oneNest had learned to crawl and walk. After a few stumbles, it was ready to start running—at the very time I was being forced to push it to a new owner.

I had wanted to link the haves and the have-nots. I had wanted to create a new business model capable of connecting the developed and less developed worlds and of blending purpose with profit.

Instead I had let down so many people, including myself and my baby in the stroller. I had not managed to show how business could be used to create substantial positive change. I had come up short. Way short.

Those final weeks would be a blur—a laborious process of cleaning up and wrapping up all of oneNest's assets, online and offline. We had to work with the distribution center in Pennsylvania to determine what to send to the company that had bought oneNest. And there were our employees. In those final days, I would tend to my remaining team with extra care.

My heart ached, wondering if the only ones who gained from this whole experiment were the investors. This is the underbelly of one-dimensional capitalism: a company like oneNest is valued not for the new markets it connected and developed, the small businesses across the world it helped, or the thousands of women and their families it lifted from poverty, but only for its financial profit. I had tried to connect social and environmental good to financial profit, but in the end, the market did not really care.

Catching my breath, I knelt down beside Diya, who was tucked snugly into her stroller, and tried not to worry. Out over the water, Lady Liberty was holding court. I had spied her for the first time from the window of the plane in 1985, on my way to my first year at Smith. I was seventeen then. When I'd looked out that plane window at the Statue of Liberty below, I'd felt hope, possibility, and wonder. Now, all these years later, I felt despair. I felt as if I'd somehow let down Lady Liberty herself and the millions of immigrants who'd gone before me. Twenty years into my grand experiment—the one my parents had warned me would never work—what, I wondered, had I accomplished?

I didn't have an answer, but I did know this: it was time to leave the United States. The United States had given me so much. It had given me my education. And experience. And Rob. And Diya. The opportunity to reach for so many dreams. But alongside the dreams had come the nightmare of 9/11. Just as 9/11 and those planes had forever changed me, they had also changed the United States. I no longer felt the safety and security I had once felt. Increasingly, I felt like an outsider. A growing number of Americans saw me as one of "those people," more readily associated with the men who flew the planes into the towers than with a friend or neighbor they'd invite to a barbecue.

Raw and vulnerable, I needed to go where I felt safe again. For me, it was time to go home.

PART IV

Imagine a New World

CHAPTER EIGHTEEN

Belonging

"Diya, Sweetie, why don't you give it a try? See all the kids running around? They love the snow. Don't you want to play with the snow?"

My two-and-a-half-year-old was standing next to a plastic Christmas tree with her arms crossed. A thin cotton dress and short haircut did not help Diya adjust to the steaming tropical heat of Singapore. She was sweating and pouting.

"No. It's *fake* snow. I want real snow. I want to go back to New York. I want to go back home, and I want Papa." Tears formed in her eyes as I kneeled and hugged her tight.

"Papa will be back soon," I said, switching to Bengali. "Papa had to go back to be with *Omma*. She is very sick, and she needs Papa. I am here with you. Come, let's go inside and get some ice cream. You are a big girl now; maybe you can get a cone all to yourself."

Moving to Singapore had not been easy. Last time I had moved between countries I was alone, carrying one suitcase. This time, it was six suitcases, a husband, a child, and a container full of stuff coming via ocean freight. I had never lived in Singapore, a tiny country at the tip of the Malaysian Peninsula boasting an exciting mix of Chinese, Indian, Malay, and Western flavors. But after 9/11 and the racial backlash against South Asians, Southeast Asia felt like a healing balm. The city felt like an ideal home with the perfect blend of everything Asian and comfort.

We moved into an apartment building close to the city's central area, bustling with shopping malls, fancy designer label stores, and high-end hotels. The relentless tropical sun meant we spent most of our life in clean, air-conditioned, indoor areas. Our lives felt scrubbed, cleaned, and put in a box with a new set of rules.

At the time, the world considered Singapore an "Asian Tiger": a high-growth economy, living proof of how a country can grow and prosper with the right balance of government policy and private sector involvement. The government had thoroughly planned the city-state, including affordable public housing, clean and effective public transportation, well-maintained nature reserves, affordable food courts serving Asian delights, and an academically focused educational system. It all seemed too good to be true.

Once we started living in this ideal city-state, however, little things start gnawing at me. No chewing gum, no spitting, no jaywalking, no disorderly behavior. So many rules, the rigidity of the system, and especially the most frequently used word: *cannot*.

"Can we have the fried rice without the egg? My daughter is allergic to eggs," I would ask the waitress at a local restaurant.

"No, cannot," she'd replied tersely.

"But why? My daughter can't eat eggs," I'd push.

"No, cannot. Order something else."

Rules were rules. Nobody bent them, even if it meant an unhappy customer. The only person who could decide to make fried rice without eggs was the restaurant owner, and nobody knew who or where he was. An invisible boss controlled the menu in the same way that the government controlled every aspect of the city-state.

What *was* allowed was the unapologetic display of wealth. Fancy cars rolled along the clean roads, lined with perfectly manicured trees and brightly colored bougainvillea bushes. Rolls Royce, Porsche, Ferrari, Lamborghini: you name it. A car in Singapore cost almost ten times what it would cost in the United States. But cars in Singapore were the badge of new wealth. Just blocks from our apartment, fancy malls and designer brand stores glistened on the main commercial thoroughfare: Isetan, Takashimaya, Cartier, Tiffany, Hermes, and others. These stores enjoyed the patronage of Singapore's wealthy as well as the wealthy from across Asia.

With its effective financial system and reputation as an Asian Tiger, Singapore rapidly approached Switzerland as a hub of global private wealth. At the time in the early 2000s, in South and Southeast Asia and the resource-rich African countries, a small group of citizens grew mind-bogglingly wealthy. It seemed that the poorer countries neighboring Singapore were producing an exceptionally rich upper class at the expense of the 99 percent in their countries. They had begun parking their wealth in this safe, clean, and efficient Switzerland of Asia. The Asian version of the wealthy 1 percent was alive and thriving in Singapore.

And Singapore itself embraced the flow of money within its borders. Large multinational corporations opened regional offices, and the government made it easy for anyone to start a business. You could register a new business online and get the approval via text message within twenty-four hours. Corporate taxes were minimal. Singapore, wrapped in efficiency and smart public policy, was indeed a paradise for the wealthy.

All this order was a far cry from our lively New York chaos of cobbled streets and corner grocers. I never believed I would miss the subway system of New York, but I did. I missed exchanging a few words of Spanish with the young man at the sidewalk stall where I used to buy flowers. I missed New York. And yet another part of me also appreciated the orderliness of Singapore. Maybe I need this in my life now, I thought. Maybe all these rules and this attention to efficiency are what a country needs to achieve effective economic growth.

Perhaps here I could bring together the lives I lived before in a safe environment. Although I was working in media again, at what I thought was a safe job at a magazine company, wheels of questions still turned in the back of my mind. I was still haunted by the elusive goal of a financial model that would work for all. I kept wondering: is it possible to use the power of finance to empower the have-nots—and to do it on a global scale?

***

For the nine years before I had Diya, I had been unable to make my mother-in-law happy. Her plans for Rob had never included a brown immigrant woman. She had tried countless times to break up our relationship, both before and after our marriage, with her dogma that mixed-race marriages simply don't work. But Rob and I had gotten married, and her discontent continued—until Diya was born.

"Thank God she got our coloring!" was the first thing Betty said to Rob, smiling when she saw Diya just minutes after she was born. Even in my half-conscious state from anesthesia, her words cut through my heart. That statement confirmed what I had known all along: Rob's mother was no different from many people I had met in America or elsewhere. Many were liberal enough to have friends from other races. But bringing someone from another race into the family and embracing the struggle that an interracial marriage signaled? Few people wanted to take that on.

Now that same feisty woman had cancer and was fighting for her life. Seeing her frail body in the wheelchair when she arrived at the Singapore airport for a visit, I was suddenly filled with love and pity. Yes, she had made my life difficult. Yet she had thought she was protecting her son, and I could identify with that impulse, misguided though it had been.

"Durreen, I want to tell you something," Rob's mother said to me one afternoon during her visit. Her barely audible words hung heavily in the air. She had gone to the botanical gardens with Diya and Rob in the morning, and now she looked exhausted. I helped her to bed, propped up her pillow, and tried to adjust her in a comfortable position so that she could breathe more easily while she rested. Her legs were bloated, and she was visibly in pain. I took the lotion from the side table and started rubbing it on her calves to bring down the swelling.

"Durreen, listen to me," she continued gently but with an urgency in her voice. I looked up from massaging her leg. She was a beautiful woman with the deepest blue eyes. Now her eyes were filled with tears, and she looked straight at me.

"I am sorry. I am so sorry for all this time." She paused. I did not know where this was coming from, and I didn't know what to say.

"I did not want you to marry Rob, but you showed me that you loved my son and that you are a good wife. I am leaving him to a good woman. Please take care of my son when I am not here." Her voice drifted off, and she did not wait for my response. She closed her eyes and turned her head in the other direction on the pillow. That was the end of our conversation.

Her statement, couched as an apology, made me feel sad and defeated. She had acknowledged my love for Rob, but she had knowingly been unkind to me. All these years I had justified her behavior toward me as either her ignorance or my overreaction. Now I learned it had been neither; instead it was driven by a complex set of emotions that perhaps she herself came to terms with only recently.

Maybe she would have been more inclusive and understanding if I had worked harder to expose her to my culture? Should I have shown interest in learning to bake American pies? Chasing the elusive inclusion in my American family led to so many maybes. I had spent my whole life thus far chasing power and inclusion, be it in family, in society, in organizations, in the system as a whole: banging at its door, trying to get to its source, getting slapped in the face when I, as a brown woman, "overstepped."

Why do humans fundamentally fear difference, whether people or ideas? Why do we fight so hard to preserve the status quo? So much of the fear of including people different from ourselves, or breaking free from the status quo, is rooted in our perception of risk. This risk perception brings out a savior attitude, where we think we know what is best for the people we want to exclude and control.

Inclusion simply means sharing power with others, no matter who or what they are. Inclusion means listening to all and embracing ideas and thoughts you may not always agree with. Inclusion means foregoing some of your own power in order to create greater social good. All this can be terrifying or exciting, depending on how you perceive risk. Having been an outsider for so long, I kept wondering why we couldn't set up systems—family systems, school systems, financial systems—with notions of inclusion written into them. As a mother, I was about to learn, more intimately than I had so far, what inclusion requires of all of us.

CHAPTER NINETEEN

Something to Fight For

"Bahu, I'm in London, waiting for my connecting flight." Rob was on his way back to Singapore after his mother's funeral, and I could hear the fatigue and sadness in his voice. He was still a fourteen-hour plane journey away from home, and now I had to drop another bombshell: I was in labor.

Lying in the hospital bed, I closed my eyes and tried to rest between contractions. When my water broke six hours earlier, I had not known whom to call. Our lives in Singapore had been so busy, with both of us traveling constantly for work and taking care of Diya, that we had not found time to make any friends. Our neighbor Priya had been kind to us since we moved in next door, and our children played together often, so I had called her. Upon hearing the news, Priya jumped into action. She called two of her friends, Indi and Parvati, who quickly mobilized to care for Diya while helping me to the hospital.

"What? How can you be in labor? You're not due for over two months!" Rob exclaimed. There was no way he would make it to Singapore in time for the birth.

This pregnancy had been a completely unexpected but bright spot in our otherwise gray lives. But it had been a difficult one from the beginning. I had not gained the weight I was supposed to gain, and

I had fainted a couple of times. And now here I was, in labor two months early.

With all of Rob's traveling to the United States to care for his ailing mother, he had not settled fully into the Singapore office of his firm. And, for my part, I had walked into a corporate nightmare. Asia's new wealth gave Western companies with global plans the opportunity to make money hand over fist. It seemed as if these companies had walked into Aladdin's forty thieves' cave and were greedily stuffing their pockets with gold and gems. Such corporations seemed to have little regard for the social and environmental compromises needed to obtain that rapid profit. The media company I worked for was very much a part of that pack. A company that touted its faith-based practices in the United States apparently kept those ethics stored away. In its Asian offices, the company was doing whatever it could to squeeze out every last penny.

I soon found myself struggling to make sense of the company's dubious business practices. As the head of the Asia business, I dug into the finances and found several "creative" accounting practices, including one by which a company avoids paying taxes to the countries in which they operate and channels money back to the United States. Before long, government authorities were raiding our company's international offices to seize documents for financial audits.

Throughout this chaotic period, I found myself arguing constantly with senior management. I refused to participate in these shady practices and believed, stubbornly, that I could influence leadership to do the same. Alas, after nine months of my trying to change their business ethics, they handed me a pink slip. For the first time in my life, I had been fired.

Getting fired from a job is never an easy pill to swallow, yet in some ways this termination felt like a triumph. I had stood up for what was right. Not for a moment did I regret my decision to stand up to corporate wrongdoing. There is no justification for any amount of profit if tainted by human or environmental costs. Years later, when the company declared bankruptcy, I felt a measure of vindication.

My termination put our lives in turmoil. We had to evacuate our corporate apartment, which threw our whole lives in Singapore into question. But job loss, a grieving husband, a move: none of it matters when you are trying to keep a baby inside your body who is determined to come out. It was as if the baby had a message for the world and she had decided that now was the time to share it.

***

I opened my eyes in the hospital room, and as the world came back into clear view, I felt excruciating pain. The door opened and a nurse walked over to me. "How are you feeling?" she inquired gently.

"What happened? I want to see my baby. Please take me to my baby," I whispered back, my throat painfully dry.

"You will see the baby. We just need to make sure you are OK. You lost a lot of blood. You need to rest now; I will call your husband."

Looking directly into the nurse's eyes, I repeated, "I want to see my baby!" and licked my dry, cracked lips. She ignored me, checking the dressing of my abdominal cut before leaving the room. Lying there with no news, I bargained with the universe: take me, but let my baby live. Please. My mind turned to Diya. What was she doing? Where was Rob?

After what felt like hours, Rob came through the doors. He had made it back from London just in time for the emergency C-section, as nurses wheeled me into the operating room. Seeing him right as the anesthesia was kicking in had felt like a dream, and I had felt so relieved.

But now? Now I was angry. "Rob, what happened with the baby? Did you see the baby?" I was vexed at him the minute he walked into my hospital room after settling Diya back in the apartment.

"I don't know. She is in intensive care in an incubator. I couldn't see much from outside the window. They won't let me inside. They won't tell me anything either." The circles under Rob's eyes looked like deep pools. With his head down, Rob stared at the floor.

Finally, on day four, doctors lifted me into a wheelchair and wheeled me slowly to the nursery. I passed rows and rows of babies, all tiny and cute and bundled up, lying peacefully in their cots. Parents stood at the window, smiling and pointing at their newborns. I felt happy for them while fighting a sinking feeling in my stomach.

The nurse stopped my wheelchair near the row of the incubators, as a doctor began the explanation I had been waiting for. "Your baby was born with a genetic disorder," he said in a clinical voice. "Your baby is only the second case Singapore has seen. You may be distressed when you see her, so we will be close by to make sure both you and the baby are safe."

The nurse went to the incubator that had a light shining directly on a tiny red baby wearing an oversized diaper. She slid up the incubator door, wrapped the baby in a blanket, and brought her over to me. The nurse bent over gingerly and placed my daughter on my lap.

The baby was tiny. She had weighed barely four pounds at birth and had lost some weight since then. Although I was pumping milk for her, she was too distressed to drink it. I could barely feel her weight. But what she lacked in weight, she made up with simple presence. She was awake, but she did not make any sound. She looked at me with shining dark eyes. They were almond-shaped, laced with thick long lashes. She looked directly at me and did not blink. She was looking into my soul, staring at me as if to say, "Where were you all these days?"

"Durreen, this child's soul has been here before," Rob's grandmother would tell me later, when she came over from Chicago to help me with Aliya. "She has a wise old soul." His grandmother, who had emigrated from Germany after World War II, had been an ally of mine in the midst of fraught family relationships. Looking at the baby in my arms now, I knew that Rob and I had picked the right name for her. Aliya: "the benevolent one," in Arabic and in Hebrew, "the journey of ascending" or "to the motherland." Aliya had arrived here with a message. I didn't know what it was yet, but this child had a mission. This benevolent one would help me ascend to new levels of self-discovery.

Slowly pulling back the blanket from Aliya's head, I saw her scalp, which was covered with thick scales like an intricate crown. Her ears were curled up like stuffed samosas, not ready for the noise of the world. The skin on her face was red and stretched, protecting the beauty underneath. I unfolded the blanket a bit more and saw a thick, shiny, shell-like skin all over her tiny body. I took her little hand into my palm. Her fingers were tiny buds.

I gingerly uncovered more. Her legs were awkwardly bent, as if still undecided about which direction to grow. Her tiny, cracked feet had made the rebellious decision to turn in, and just like her fingers, her toes were little buds. She looked like a beautiful mermaid, one not yet ready for her time on the land. She was still growing, trying to find her way between scales and skin, tail and legs, fins and arms.

I wrapped my little baby back up in her blanket and held her tightly next to my chest while inhaling the scent of petroleum jelly on her body. I kissed her tiny crown of a head and whispered, "You are beautiful. You are my beautiful mermaid baby." I had no tears. I was filled with love. I was also overwhelmed with the realization that I would need to struggle to ensure both Aliya's health and her inclusion in a world that may not want to embrace her.

I finally awoke from my trance of love and awe when a nurse asked if I was OK. "Yes, I am absolutely fine," I said. "Thank you for taking care of my baby. Can you tell me what is happening with her care? Also, should she be under that light? It looks like it's hurting her skin."

The nurses looked at each other, and the pediatrician jumped in. "Baby Aliya is what is known as a 'collodion baby," he told me. "Her condition is harlequin ichthyosis. These babies are born in a shell of a tight, shiny membrane that looks like plastic wrap. Ichthyosis is a genetic condition in which the skin doesn't produce moisture. The skin is very tight, and that is why some of her body parts did not grow, and why she cannot close her eyes. The body knows that the skin is not working, so it tries to fix it. That is why the skin keeps on regenerating. That's also why she has scales which continually flake off. There is no cure for this. It is a lifelong condition."

The pediatrician very patiently explained all this to me with a face devoid of emotion. I took it all in, saying nothing.

"Here, let me take the baby from you," whispered the head nurse as she leaned over to take the baby from my arms. "She needs to get back in the incubator. She is a clever baby. Look at how she is looking at us and listening to us!"

I gently kissed Aliya's forehead and made a promise. I would always be there for her. I would make sure the world embraced her. She and her sister were my heart and soul. Making the systems of the world more inclusive and accessible to those who have been kept out: the task before me now seemed more urgent than ever.

***

A group of mothers stared at Aliya and frowned. They were speaking rapidly in hushed Mandarin, their irritation intelligible even to someone who did not speak the language. The mothers held their children's hands tightly. Some toddlers were curious and others petrified; meanwhile, their mothers judged me for bringing Aliya to their children's playgroup.

At eight months old, Aliya was starting to crawl and was full of curiosity. Her hair was slowly growing in patches of curls, making headway among the cracks of the scales on her scalp. By gently massaging a combination of salicylic acid and coconut oil into her scalp each day, I would try to make room for any hair follicle in sight. I had to be careful, though, as a significant portion of her skull bone had not developed, and I could feel her brain throbbing under the scaly scalp.

Aliya's eyes were shiny and curious, sparkling from the eye drops I had to put in every half hour so that they didn't dry out. She took in every detail of the world around her. Her body was constantly shedding skin, up to two cups every day. It was a fight between me and the universe to make her skin function, to make my little mermaid ready for her life on this Earth. I researched her condition endlessly, looking for a glimmer of hope, a treatment, a cure. I made one concoction after another, covering her small body with every kind of emollient to try to stop the next cycle of scales. Aliya would just look at me intently as I massaged her skin with medicated lotions, ending with a thick layer of paraffin to keep in the artificially created moisture on her body for the next half hour. Over and over, I repeated the routine. But new scales would soon resurface, establishing their dominance until they fell off to make way for new ones.

But the minute I put her in her bath, my little mermaid baby would reclaim her body. The water would make her skin smooth and soft, and Aliya would smile her toothless smile, her eyes shining. I would slowly scrub off her scales and tell her, "I will make the world ready for you. You will make the rest of us realize that we are incomplete. You will complete us all." I would let her play in her natural habitat as long as possible before I had to bring her back to land.

Rob and I took Aliya to every doctor in Singapore who would see us, and my world condensed to focus on feeding Aliya, taking care of her skin, and setting up supply chains for her medications from across the world: medicated lotions from the United States, Ayurvedic lotions from India, dead sea salts from Israel, traditional Chinese medicine from Hong Kong. Diya would join in when I gently massaged Aliya's hands and toes to nudge her fingers and toes to grow. Diya could not understand why other children ran away from the perfect little sister she loved so much.

When I took Aliya out, the world treated her as an untouchable, unacceptable for society. Strangers would ask me outright: "Why did you bring her out in public?" I questioned myself when I heard this. Was I harming Aliya by exposing her to the world? Or was I simply exposing the difficulty people have relating to those who are different? Had we all forgotten how to embrace and include?

I began to ask myself: what do you do when someone doesn't know how to include others? Plain and simple: you take a deep breath, and then you educate them. You don't ignore. You don't cry. You don't get angry. You just educate. Education is always the path to truth.

So I designed a postcard with flower artwork and these words on it, one side in English and the other in Mandarin:

Thank you for your curiosity about my child's well-being. My child was born with ichthyosis, a rare genetic disorder. My goal is to educate the public so that people with ichthyosis are not subjected to staring, pointing, and teasing. Ichthyosis is a skin disorder that causes severely dry skin. It is not contagious. It is a lifelong condition for which there is no cure. Children with ichthyosis take lots of baths and use lots of lotion to keep their skin as comfortable as possible. We hope you will find it in your heart to be compassionate to my daughter and anyone else you meet with ichthyosis or any other visible skin disorder.

On that day at the playgroup, I handed out postcards to the mothers talking about Aliya in Mandarin and pulling their children away from her.

"Here, please read the card," I said. "Please don't be scared."

They shook their heads. I repeated, "Please take it. I am asking you, as one mother to another."

One by one, they hesitantly took copies of the postcard. They read. They looked at each other, and they looked at Aliya. Then they looked at me. They apologized, their apologies covered with embarrassment.

"We're very sorry . . . it is just that—"

I interrupted. "You don't need to explain," I said, and smiled. "Thank you for having open minds." They gingerly brought their children over to Aliya to say hello.

Education was working. Slowly and painfully, inclusion was happening. But it was a process that needed to be repeated over and over. I ended up writing a version of that postcard as a letter to the residents of an apartment building to which we had moved and where children and adults were being cruel to both Aliya and Diya. I printed out more than six hundred copies of the letter, one for each apartment in the complex. I went downstairs and inserted an envelope into each of the mailboxes. I had a lump in my throat. I had no tears. Education is about changing minds and hearts. It is about rendering fear and anger into courage.

CHAPTER TWENTY

New Systems, from Scratch

"I was a banker. I was a social entrepreneur. I was a media executive. Now I am a professor. Here I am, teaching all of you, brilliant minds from all over the world, about social innovation. Do you know why?"

I always started my classes with this question. A roomful of graduate students at the Lee Kuan Yew School of Public Policy at the National University of Singapore would look back at me, waiting.

Soon after we moved to Singapore, at a Smith College gathering, I met the dean of the school of public policy at the National University of Singapore. His wife was a Smith alum. Before I knew it, I was an adjunct professor, teaching a class combining economic development and finance with social innovation and entrepreneurship. Students worldwide came to this university to learn the magic of public policy from a country that had been transformed from a sleepy port city to an Asian economic tiger by the strength of its public policy and the leadership of a visionary politician and lawyer, Lee Kuan Yew.

I looked across the room full of students, curious but reserved. "Well? Any guesses?" I probed. Slowly a few answers started coming. "Because we need to innovate in a society to move forward equitably?" an Indian woman said, bravely taking the first stab.

"Because governments need to innovate?" followed a Chinese man.

I smiled. "You are both right. But it is more than that. Many of you will join public service, so you will have the power to change the course of your country," I told them. "I want you to remember that three sectors of society—public policy, civil society, and the private sector—come together at an important nexus. This is the 'social innovation zone.' This is the zone where it is possible to create social equity and justice in a sustainable way. One manifestation of that goal is a new type of entity called a 'social enterprise'—or an 'impact enterprise.' In this course you will learn how to use this social innovation zone effectively to address some of the most pressing needs of the world."

At this point in the mid-2000s, social enterprise as a concept was in its early stages. Bill Drayton was popularizing it through his nonprofit advocacy organization, Ashoka, but the concept was limited to the nonprofit sector. Defining social entrepreneurs as individuals and organizations working to meet human needs within the nonprofit sector seemed too limited to me. If we were going to use the term *entrepreneurship*—in essence, the creation of business—we needed to use the power of the financial system with a strong base of sustainability in all three areas: financial, social, and environmental.

Social enterprises—or impact enterprises, as businesses creating positive impact came to be known—require a financially sustainable business model that addresses social or environmental needs. Financial sustainability would free businesses from dependence on philanthropy and vulnerability to the whims of donors. In turn, the financial system had to learn to value these organizations' positive social and environmental contributions. The financial system had to become inclusive enough to place a financial value on social good.

The concept of driving social innovation through business was catching on in the United States, where the culture celebrates and encourages entrepreneurship. Yet the environment in Asia was very different. I now found myself teaching public policy to students from countries with wildly different systems: capitalist, quasi-capitalist, socialist, democratic, and authoritarian. Most of these students had been accustomed to memorizing theories and ideologies. They had not been encouraged to think critically or to question systems.

And I was determined that this course not just educate students but create new thinkers. Education had opened my eyes to new types of power, and it had given me power. I was determined to use this power for others. To fully convey the challenge and the opportunity to my students in Singapore I needed to step back and consider what I was teaching and how.

I thought back to my childhood in postwar Bangladesh and how international development organizations dictated how our country would be rebuilt. I remembered civil society organizations and government working hand in hand to create a functioning economy, with only a small role for the private sector in postwar development. This dynamic made the country perpetually dependent on foreign aid. I recalled my own mixed emotions while giving alms to the poor on Muslim holidays. For the recipient of the donations, our charity only created a sense of dependency, with little hope of rising above it.

I thought back to my teenage years in the Philippines, where a group of wealthy families, some with ancestry going back to the Spanish and American colonial days, controlled the country's economy with a nod from the government. Civil society had a weak voice, and ordinary people's frustration with the rich getting richer boiled over in the People Power revolution. People grew angry with governmental abuses of power and plutocrats, and the anger that erupted toppled the government.

I thought back to the United States, where I had seen economic growth fueled by entrepreneurship—albeit shaped by gender and race constraints—and the power of finance to make it all move. On Wall Street, I had joined a financial machine helping companies grow enormously. But the only type of return rewarded in that system was financial return. A company had to maximize profit for its shareholders, so in this purely capitalist system, the only players who mattered were shareholders and consumers. Both fuel the growth of the company: one by financing the company and the other by buying its products. The well-being of other stakeholders—employees, suppliers, society itself, the environment—did not matter. What mattered in these equations was producing a product efficiently with keen focus on maximizing financial profit.

I remembered all the finance and operations classes in my graduate studies, during which professors pounded into us the notion of efficiency. Investors would reward us, we learned, according to our ability to make products quickly and cheaply. Our courses never mentioned the social and environmental cost of this efficiency.

And I thought of Singapore, the country in which I was now living and where a powerful government set policy from the top down, for the sake of efficiency. The process worked well for efficient economic growth. But what was the impact on society?

There were so many models for how to develop a country. But could we look at proliferation of impact enterprise as another model for inclusive growth? Could small businesses that create positive social impact be the engine of bottom-up growth? And could financial markets play a role in that journey to sustainable growth? I wondered if I could make a case for a new model: one that would be more inclusive and innovative, and one that would value social and environmental effectiveness and stakeholder engagement and voice as highly as efficiency.

***

The answer started unfolding in my head as I reflected on my career as a practitioner, pored over the academic literature, and developed and tested ideas with my students. I became convinced that the answer lay at the nexus of government, the private sector, and civil society. Each had a role to play in social innovation. Pulling together elements of each, we could create a model where small businesses with positive impact could grow and thrive.

First, the government, or the public sector, needed to be the catalyst; it needed to incentivize businesses to proactively create social and environmental good and not just penalize them when some major disaster happened. Second, companies in the private sector needed to measure the impact of their work on society and the environment while still pursuing financial profit. The markets that financed these businesses needed to acknowledge and value the companies' social and environmental returns. Finally, civil society— communities and nonprofit organizations focused on social justice— needed to embrace financial sustainability as a prerequisite to enable impact enterprises to achieve social justice. The public sector, private sector, and civil society all had to share power rather than lording it over each other. Like the three legs of a stool, they all had to be balanced for society to flourish.

And I was growing more convinced that the system could only achieve balance if small businesses, sitting in the social innovation zone, remained vibrant. Mission-driven businesses needed an opportunity to grow in a way that celebrated and encouraged the positive impact embedded in their business models. At the same time, more traditional micro, small, and medium businesses could be transformed by having the DNA of positive impact injected in them. The common factor in making this happen would be an impact-driven financial infrastructure. We needed government, civil society, and the private sector to work together to make this happen.

I had seen firsthand how deeply small businesses impact communities, how their positive impact silently ripples through the financial system, and how rarely they are rewarded for it. My mother understood the power of small businesses while running her own clandestine bakery and helping business owners in our community. Through her, I saw the power that small businesses hold and the positive outcomes they create. As she helped other entrepreneurs, they not only grew their businesses and created jobs but also began giving opportunities to women in their supply chain and embracing their own daughters' education.

At Grameen Bank, I saw how giving microloans to women in remote villages in Bangladesh positively impacted their families, communities, and the environment. My clients became empowered by the money they earned from their microbusinesses, be it selling milk from their cows, eggs from their chickens, or shawls they wove.

With their earnings, they could feed their families, afford healthcare, and send their children to school. I saw women planting vegetable patches and trees and putting in proper latrines by their houses. Women who had been too shy to look me in the eye became confident businesswomen. Before my eyes, they slowly but surely gained power. Not only did they earn money from their small businesses; they earned respect and validation from a society that previously had not valued them.

Then, at oneNest, I saw how women entrepreneurs could grow their businesses by having access to markets for their products. The thousands of small businesses we brought to the global market during the early days of the internet made me marvel. We sold beautiful handmade vegetable-dyed tablecloths and napkins from India, aromatic cinnamon stick-decorated candleholders from Indonesia, stuffed toys made from organic cotton from Sri Lanka, recycled glass jewelry from Mexico, naturally mud-dyed cloth from Ghana, and natural soy candles from the United States. The list went on. Loving hands from local communities made all these products using resources thoughtfully sourced in harmony with the local environment.

More than 90 percent of all companies around the world are small businesses. They form the backbone of every single economy. These enterprises are deeply embedded in their local communities and are able to bring social innovation and inclusion to what has been called "the last mile"—the farthest reaches of human society, making sure nobody is left out. They have incentives to provide employment opportunities and goods and services that help that community, because they belong to it. The community is their livelihood, so they have a stake in supporting it; in turn, the community ensures that the business thrives. This symbiotic relationship reduces the risk of failure for the business.

Despite being the engines of an economy, small businesses—a majority of which are women-owned—have never been fully valued for the role they play in the social and environmental fabric of their communities. Worldwide and across the board, small businesses struggle to access the funding they need in order to grow. Only 10 percent of female entrepreneurs have the capital necessary to expand their businesses. Women-owned businesses often languish because they do not receive the necessary capital.

To create a truly inclusive system, we needed to validate and reward all the contributions that these small businesses make in the community: social, environmental, and financial. The impact of the flow of money is easy to measure. Social and environmental impacts, while hard to measure, are equally powerful. How could we demonstrate that to the market?

We had to think expansively, I told my students—expansively enough to create a system that was more just. This might mean building new a system from scratch.

CHAPTER TWENTY-ONE

The Meaning of Impact

Imagine if soft drink producers had to pay a higher price for the water they used in water-scarce countries. How would that change their behavior and their pricing in places like Mexico? And what if these massive companies then had to foot the medical bills arising from the 40 percent increase in diabetes their products created in these same communities? Would that make them realize that it is not worth the cost—environmental, social, and financial—to use up the little water in the community to produce sugary drinks? Would that make them think differently about how to produce soft drinks in Mexico? How would their shareholders react to all this? In this case, the well-being of all the company's major stakeholders—the consumer, the community, and the environment—are being ignored for the sake of a single stakeholder: the investor.

I walked through examples like these with my students because I needed them to understand: it didn't have to be this way. By then, in the mid-2000s, environmental awareness was slowly making headway into people's consciousness as the devastating effects of climate change unfolded all around us. Global temperatures were rising measurably, while certain emerging countries like China, India, and Brazil were overtaking the United States and Europe as emitters of greenhouse gases. The summer months were hotter, drier, and longer, and wildfires raged more frequently and with more ferocity across the globe. Arctic animals were endangered, as over a million square kilometers of sea ice disappeared annually. The oceans were rising and eating away at the low-lying coastal land of many islands and countries.

Many of my students came from countries that were experiencing the wrath of climate change firsthand. They already understood the impact that the degradation of climate was having on society. More than 1.3 billion people were already living on deteriorating agricultural land and were at risk of failed harvests, worsening hunger, poverty, and displacement. The UN had estimated that 80 percent of people displaced by climate change were women. Low-income women in developing countries are often trapped in subsistence living, which makes it harder for them to cope with shocks. Without action on climate change, 100 million people could be forced into poverty by 2030.

How could we slow this environmental degradation? Corporations held much of the power to mitigate climate change—but they needed encouragement to do the right thing. They needed a combination of government regulation and incentives from financial markets. My students were the future leaders who could go back to their countries and influence policy decisions to address these challenges in an innovative way.

By the time regulators catch companies polluting the earth or discriminating against a group of people, it's too late. The damage has already been done, and any penalty exacted is typically not enough to influence corporate decision-making. In the existing system, companies do not internalize these negative impacts as a financial cost for their business. They are free to maintain the status quo without absorbing the true cost of their injurious practices. But it doesn't have to be this way, I told my students.

The exclusion of entire demographics of people and unsustainable environmental and societal practices exact a tremendously high cost—and who pays the price? In the current system, society pays the price when a company pollutes, discriminates, and creates harm. Because the cost of that negative impact isn't quantified in dollars, the company doesn't suffer and their malpractice can continue.

On the flip side, if a company is creating *positive* impacts, the company rarely receives a financial benefit for these actions. Could we envision a way to value these positive impacts to reward companies for these practices? Could the government catalyze this behavior? And could the financial markets embrace and value this positive impact?

I turned this question back to my students. "Is this the system you want?" I asked. "Do we want to sustain the system we have today, full of top-down solutions that benefit a small group of capital owners? Or can we create a system that values, measures, and rewards positive impacts on people and the environment?"

As we discussed this unusual perspective, their questions began to flow. How do you change a system? Who holds power? Is it the government? The people? Large corporations? Investors? I smiled. Education was working—for all of us. As I walked around the classroom, absorbing the students' curiosity and sharing my own analysis, I felt many tiny light bulbs going on in my head. There had to be a way to harness the power of the financial system to make it work for all. There had to be a related infrastructure that could carry out the work. Looking around the classroom, I put into words a thought that had been keeping me awake at night: "wealth holds within it the power of inclusion and sustainability."

Looking back through history at the building of empires—Greeks, Romans, Mongols, Moghuls, Ottoman, Portuguese, Spanish, Dutch, British, French, German, and countless others—we see that the leaders' ambition had always been driven by the accumulation of wealth, which went hand in hand with power. The European colonizers' conquest of the world focused on extracting wealth from colonies in the Global South, reinforcing the colonizers' power and allowing them to maintain control of the source of that wealth. The power of wealth to exclude, divide, and abuse has been with us for millennia. What if we switched the equation and used that wealth to create positive change instead?

This was early 2007. Financial markets were flying high, and Asian economies were growing at an exhilarating clip. And yet in these same Asian countries, more than 1.4 billion people were still living on less than $1.25 a day, with barely enough to eat and limited or no access to education, electricity, and health services. At a time when the global financial assets were valued at more than $100 trillion, nobody was interested in hearing about inclusive economic growth. Who needed inclusive markets when exclusion was generating so much wealth?

And yet the global financial boom was precisely a reason to push on this topic. In flush times, when stocks soar and money seems to grow on trees, it's easy to lose sight of the other ways markets impact our lives. Why weren't we valuing all the various ways that companies impact the world?

As a former social entrepreneur, I knew that for-profit companies that need to raise capital to expand are at the mercy of venture capitalists who tend to care less about positive impact and more about greater output with less cost. At oneNest, for example, our investors measured us next to other marketplaces using the same yardstick of inputs, activities, and outputs. Using that yardstick, they judged that we had a challenging business model: we paid more for the goods we resold (*inputs*); we expended more labor to make the sales (*activities*); and we did not charge a high enough price for the end product (*outputs*) to make a large enough profit for the investors' liking.

What the investors did not measure was the positive impact of our practices on our suppliers and on the environment: our *outcomes*. Ensuring this positive social and environmental impact required so much work. To build an inclusive supply base involving groups of people who had never held formal jobs before or produced products on a large scale came with a financial cost. We had to train our suppliers to create products efficiently while also adhering to global product quality standards. And the cost of production was higher, as the products could not be mass-produced but had to be made by small groups spread across various villages. Insisting on natural and organic materials added costs.

We were aware of all of this, and yet we chose to run the business this way because we cared above all about the outcome: the employment and empowerment of thousands of women around the world. This was where oneNest would have benefited from a different yardstick. None of our competitors could come close to us on this measurement. Yet since investors did not have a yardstick to measure outcomes, they did not value oneNest's full impact.

We had been caught between a rock and a hard place. We could not squeeze producers for cheaper products without sacrificing the very impact we had set out to create, but our customers were not willing to pay more for the products. The customers liked the stories behind the products, but they were not willing to pay a premium for the products on account of the impact. As a result, we never measured well on the only existing yardstick at the time: maximum financial return for our investors.

As painful as it was to learn that lesson, I was convinced now that it didn't have to be this way. I wanted—I needed—to find a way to measure the value of outcomes. Maybe entrepreneurs didn't need to bend over backward to fit into investors' narrow framework after all. Maybe *investors* were the ones who needed to change; maybe they needed to change the frameworks they used to assess companies' worth. And maybe we could reinvent finance itself to make this possible.

***

Thus began my quest to create a science around measuring impact. I began researching and reading everything I could find, morning to night.

I thought back to my time at Grameen and to a summer I had spent at BRAC, the Bangladesh Rural Advancement Committee, an organization born after Bangladesh's independence war to assist in the recovery efforts that had grown to become the largest NGO in the world. Why did organizations evaluate outcomes with no regard to the balance of efficiency and effectiveness? Why did the nonprofit and civil society world only look at "monitoring and evaluating" projects retrospectively, rather than projecting future impacts the way financial models projected future financial returns? Why, for that matter, was impact only measured qualitatively and not quantified or given a monetary value?

Every week I began my classes with a conceptual debate. "So what is impact?" I asked my class one afternoon.

Teaching an afternoon class in a tropical climate is not an easy task, because you have to fight against the powerful after-lunch food coma. The Asian practice of eating a hot lunch of rice with various curries was a sure prompt for a good afternoon nap. So I'd walk directly up to students and pepper them with thought-provoking ideas and questions. Together we managed to keep naptime at bay.

In response to my question I saw a few knowing smiles, and hands shot up. "It's when someone or something does good; you have been telling us that," said one of the students who usually kept quiet.

"Well, we have been talking about how companies can do good, but we have also discussed examples of companies doing bad. With that in mind, then, what is impact?" I saw the puzzled, lost looks. I continued. "Impact is simply the change one creates in the world. That change can be good or bad. The more difficult question is: How do we assign value to this positive or negative impact?"

The financial markets currently value companies based on their current and expected future financial profits, I told my students. The financial markets are also good at factoring risk into the valuation of a company, rewarding companies whose financial returns are the least at risk. This risk factor can dramatically change the value of a company with the change of just a few numbers in a financial model. Then I posed the question: "But can the markets value impact?"

My question was met with silence. I was now off the deep end for these students; I could almost hear their silent prayers that these questions wouldn't appear on the midterm. I kept going. "To value something is simply to give it worth," I said. "That worth can be financial, but that is not the only kind of worth. And the financial worth is only what everyone agrees on; no metric exists outside of people. Think about it: a dollar is just a piece of paper until everyone agrees it has value. The government has a role to play as well. The government can influence the value society places on a dollar through policy. However, in a free financial market, even the government cannot mandate the value of a dollar. The people determine its value."

The financial world loves to quantify and give monetary value to ideas, products, and companies, I told them. That is one type of value. But if you look at the social and environmental impacts that we had discussed in class, you'd see that our current financial system wasn't assigning any value to positive and negative impacts at all.

I could see the class was with me. We were making this journey together, which felt good. I continued. "The legal system or the government will sometimes put a value on negative environmental or social impact retrospectively. If a company violates a regulation, they are fined for that wrongdoing to prevent such behavior again. So the government determines the financial value of the company's bad behavior. As for civil society, it 'measures' impact qualitatively but does not attempt to quantify it. In order to change the behavior of companies and the financial system, we need to incentivize and reward positive impacts—and punish negative impact. We need to be able to assign a value to the full range of impacts created by a company. It all begins with measuring impact."

To help the class visualize this, I described a scenario. "When you build a hospital, once it is up and running, you may think your work is complete. But your job as the hospital operator or financier of that hospital has just begun. The positive impact is not only about the number of hospital beds you have or how modern your equipment is; it is ultimately about the care the patients receive, the livelihoods created for your employees, and even the way you treat the waste that you are creating. So it is not only about how *efficiently* the hospital treats a greater number of patients; it is also about how *effectively* the hospital provides holistic and equitable care and serves its other stakeholders."

I stopped and pointed to the board. "See how this example follows the impact value chain logic: input → activity → output → outcome."

It was all coming together for the students—and, frankly, for me as well. The power of these ideas was launching me into a new sphere of defiance. To focus on the impact of companies meant taking on an unsustainable system that had for far too long attached value to only one element: financial return.

"So if care is accessible and affordable for patients, and if patients are treated equitably, with attention and respect regardless of their race, gender, creed, or economic condition: then couldn't we say that the hospital is operating more effectively than a comparable hospital that fills more hospital beds but turns away the poor?"

I paused. The faces of the students told me that they were getting it. The furrowed brows, the squinting eyes, and the tightening lips told me that they were starting to question what they knew about efficiency and to think about balancing it with fairness, justice, and effectiveness. They were learning that changing the questions you ask—about power, money, impact, and what matters in the end—will lead you to different answers.

CHAPTER TWENTY-TWO

Build a New Model

The fundamental problem with our current system was that the intangible qualities that make a business good for society could not be measured and converted to a financial value. If customers are not willing to pay a premium price for the social and environmental good created by a business, entrepreneurs will constantly face financing challenges, and large corporations will continuously engage in a race to the bottom, sacrificing positive social impact to decrease costs. We have simply not been taught to value positive impact. Our financial system, which is overtrained on efficiency, will view a less efficient business model as less valuable even if it creates better outcomes for society or the planet. Valuing the unvalued and undervalued required challenging the assumptions embedded in our current systems.

So many questions about building a new financial system for inclusion remained. How can we value impact? How can the cost of creating this positive impact be allocated across various stakeholders? How is impact related to risk, and can positive social impact help mitigate financial risks?

When I was running my own business, I was so busy just trying to keep oneNest alive that I did not have time to ask these kinds of questions. But now, with some distance, I realized these were questions not just for a single company, my students, or me but for society as a whole.

As I probed deeper, I came across the concept of "blended value," developed by a former social worker, Jed Emerson. I assigned his paper "The Blended Value Map" to my class, challenging them to imagine what blending the financial, social, and environmental notions of value might look like. What would it mean for society as a whole to recognize blended value and internalize it in the financial system?

Like a hunter crouched in the woods, I tracked down instances of blended value in the wild. Finding a way to measure blended value, I hoped, might be the key to a just world that would value women, underserved communities, and the environment to the tremendous extent they all deserved.

With so many dots connecting in my mind, I had to get my thoughts down on paper. To test and begin disseminating these ideas around valuing impact, I needed a case study to work through. I decided to focus my investigation on the systems of one country in particular and to apply what I was learning to that context.

I had left that country as a defiant girl, struggling to be heard. Now I would go back to Bangladesh—this time with a loud voice, still defiant but full of optimism that we could build a new, inclusive financial system.

***

During the last few decades while I had been away, Bangladesh had been slowly breaking free from the clutches of top-down economic development theories. Civil society organizations like Grameen Bank and BRAC as well as the newly emerging private-sector garment industry were helping the country embrace the financial inclusion of women from lower economic strata. My frequent trips to Bangladesh to care for my ailing parents allowed me to become reacquainted with the country and explore the ideas I had been developing through my teaching and research.

Now was the moment to test my theory that we could value all stakeholders in a new financial system. What better way to explore these ideas than through sharing my writing with Bangladeshi readers? They were used to being a Petri dish of economic growth theories. They deserved a chance to develop economic ideas endogenously, fully rooted in their own context rather than imposed by international development organizations, the vestiges of former colonial power.

The largest English-language newspaper in Bangladesh, the *Daily Star*, agreed to publish a series of my opinion pieces. I began writing articles on leadership and on how financial markets could place a value on human and environmental rights instead of solely on financial gain.

I wrote and wrote and wrote. I wrote for myself. I wrote for my daughters. I wrote for everyone who did not have a voice. Soon my writing began creating a stir. I started hearing comments and whispers in response to my op-eds.

I felt glad that my writing made people uncomfortable, because I believe that comfort is compliance. Compliance is silence. Discomfort makes us wake up and make noise.

Hungry for an audience beyond Bangladesh and Singapore, I soon started a blog called *Conscious Capitalism*. There I mused about the ways capitalism can be a force for good and how we can harness its power for social and environmental benefit. My blog started getting traffic. People started talking about it. I began to wonder if we could speak into being a new system, one where everybody mattered and everybody belonged.

I had always found it intriguing that people viewed finance as the purview of a handful of experts, almost exclusively men. Yet no matter what the men in suits who guarded these secrets wanted everyone to believe, I knew finance was just a mixture of estimates, human psychology, and educated guesses about the future.

This line of thinking led me to the work of Abraham Maslow, a psychologist who, in the 1940s, published his now well-known rubric known as the hierarchy of needs. While this approach had its share of critiques, I saw value in his framework for classifying needs. Meeting the needs of an individual seemed to be a good analog for creating a positive social impact. I used it to imagine an organization's needs as parallel to an individual's needs. Unlike what the economist Milton Friedman claimed decades prior, a company's need is not only to maximize profit for its investors, just as an individual's need is not only to maximize their wealth. The sustainable success of an organization or happiness of an individual is more complex than that, involving many layers of discovery and the numerous stakeholders that come together to ensure the success of an organization.

Maslow's hierarchy of needs mapped the human's journey to self-actualization by starting with physiological needs and progressing to psychological needs, with the ultimate step being self-actualization. What if I could replicate this progression for a company and find a way to measure each step of the journey?

Weaving these threads together, I designed an impact assessment pyramid to demonstrate how a company can become "self-actual-ized" and manifest a mission of positive impact while achieving financial sustainability. The layers of the impact assessment pyramid traced a company's progression in increasing order of its scale of impact on the outside world: the company's mission, its financial impact, followed by its social impact, its environmental impact, and finally its community impact. Each layer of the pyramid required inclusion of women and other marginalized groups of people as a key factor of success.

This assessment framework presented the perfect opportunity to build women into a vision for economic activity and finally give them the representation they deserved. Women had been neglected for far too long as a potential solution to sustainable economic development, and women's voices had not been valued in the financial markets. I wanted to change that. I started trying out these theories on the readers of my blog posts and op-eds.

Soon students were dropping by my office, eager to learn more about measuring social and environmental good. I would spend excited hours with my students in front of the whiteboard, puzzling through how to connect all the dots. The word kept spreading. Before

I knew it, students were rolling up their sleeves and going deep into the research with me.

As my research into impact assessment progressed, I became bolder. In academic papers and on my blog, I wrote fiery words against the myopic pursuit of financial returns and how it was leaving behind a path of destruction. Complete neglect of societal and environmental justice, by people with power and wealth, simply could not end well.

As the global financial system began to crack in the run-up to the 2008 crisis, those of us who had warned about the need to value factors other than the bottom line began to see our concerns playing out in real time. Like Cassandra of Greek mythology who prophesied coming destruction and was ignored, we were not listened to. A financial system cannot thrive at the expense of the well-being of others. It was only a matter of time before the bubble of greed burst.

CHAPTER TWENTY-THREE

Another One Bites the Dust

A successful global financial system is like a massive party. Fueled by excess, reaching profit-induced ecstatic highs, the party might seem like it will go on forever. By 2007, Wall Street was creating newer and more complex financial products. Investors were buying and selling those products and getting richer in the process. One such product was called a derivative. On paper, derivatives seem like crazy math equations. But put simply, a derivative is a contract between two parties in which they agree to exchange payments based on the value of some other financial product. These underlying financial products could be bonds, commodities, interest rates, currencies—anything, really. And derivatives allowed investors to place bets on the values of any of these.

So Wall Street was basically acting like a giant casino, and the players were justifying their gambling with sophisticated equations. A tiny portion of the global population—less than 1 percent, who controlled over 90 percent of global wealth—were feverishly pushing the envelope in the single-minded pursuit of creating ever greater amounts of wealth.

The casino reached its peak of excess when financial markets began gambling with residential mortgages in the United States. Residential mortgages, bank loans for home purchases, have played a beneficial role in enabling homeownership for many Americans.

These were people who worked hard to buy their first home with a mortgage. But now, thanks to the trading of derivatives, many borrowers were pulled into the labyrinth of a financial casino they hadn't even known existed.

Once people started trading derivatives on a mortgage, the loan no longer belonged to the bank from which the individual originally borrowed. Loans to American homeowners were packaged into thousands of new financial products and sold to other financial institutions, and then resold to others. The passing of the parcel continued. In the process, those in the 1 percent who were creating, selling, and buying these derivatives were making a ton of money.

This concept—bundling together a group of loans into a new financial product—is known as a collateralized loan obligation, or CLO. In purely financial terms, these CLOs are innovative solutions to the problem of risk. Diversification of loans—combining many different loans into a single pool—has the potential to reduce the risk to investors.

But any innovation can be a force for either good or evil, depending on the intentions and actions of those who utilize them. CLOs made some people very rich, and they temporarily gave access to capital to people who, in normal times, would not have had it. Many buyers had their home loans approved even though they didn't have the capacity to repay those loans.

The whole arrangement was unsustainable, and the house of cards came crashing down in 2008. Newspapers and the internet overflowed with news that people could not pay their home loans. The complicated chain of financial products whose value relied on these loans became worthless. Wealth evaporated. Investment banks failed. And many of the world's largest banks—those who had gambled the most—were bailed out by a US government fearing a total global economic collapse. The party was suddenly, painfully, over.

Excessive risk-taking by banks, combined with a bursting housing bubble in the United States, pulled the global financial market into crisis. Literally overnight, Lehman Brothers, one of the most prestigious and longest-lived Wall Street firms, collapsed. Access to credit for Lehman dried up, and the domino effect of that collapse was unstoppable. The market panicked. Everyone started running toward the exit to avoid the blaze.

A party, a casino, a bubble, dominos, fire: no matter the metaphor, the global financial crisis had terrible real-world effects, leaving millions evicted from their homes with their lives destroyed. The Great Recession of 2008 was the most severe global economic downturn since the Great Depression of the 1920s, and it spread far beyond the United States, where it began. By that time, global financial markets were so connected—and toxic bundles of CLOs had changed hands so many times across time zones—that Europe got pulled into the crisis. Greece was the first country to be engulfed in economic crisis, followed quickly by banking failures in Iceland. Economists estimate that the financial crisis led to the loss of trillions of dollars from the global economy. The economic shock resulted in unprecedented job losses and a sharp decline in demand for consumer products in the United States and developed markets. The domino effect would continue.

Those of us who had lived through a few of these dips in the financial market—Black Monday in 1987, the post–Gulf War recession in 1990, the post-9/11 panic in 2001—knew how it felt. You see the slow-motion panic in the market and in everyone around you. You hope that somehow you will come out of it unscathed, but that rarely happens. The market controlled by the 1 percent affects the 99 percent. The greed that keeps creating these crises leaves no one untouched. While the 1 percent will not share their wealth with the rest, they have a way of sharing their misery with all.

The tsunami of the financial crisis hit the shores of Asia hard. Many Asian banks followed the US banks, dragged into the crisis just like every other bank linked to the market. As I read news article after news article, my rage conjured one word over and over again: hubris. The overconfidence of these men—for the CEOs of the banks and mortgage companies were nearly all men—and their unadulterated pursuit of profit had brought the world's financial system to a screeching halt. And the 99 percent would be the ones to suffer most.

**

The crisis soon hit home in a personal way. Rob, Diya, Aliya, and I were gathering for our nightly family dinner. Diya was now six going on sixteen. She had taken on the role of the older sister and protector of Aliya. Aliya was two and a half and talking nonstop. She was very aware of her condition, and despite the physical and social challenges, she was becoming a confident little girl.

"Diya, shall I mix your food for you—the rice and dal?" I asked as I served chicken curry with lentils and rice.

"Nope. I can do it," Diya chirped as she started mixing her food, showing Aliya how to mix hers. Diya was chattering away, very focused on trying to eat with her fingers, the traditional Bengali way she had learned from me and refined on many visits to her grandparents in Dhaka. Aliya was trying to eat from her bowl, but most of it was winding up on the floor. Rob was very quiet, looking distracted and withdrawn. He pushed around the little food he had on his plate.

Finally, he broke his silence. "Diya, guess what? I can come and teach math at your school. We got a note from the school asking for parent volunteers, and I responded!" Rob smiled, leaning over to ruffle Diya's hair.

Diya squealed. "Yay, Dad! You will come to my class?"

Rob nodded his head and repeated, "Every week, two times a week."

I was confused. "Rob, what do you mean you can volunteer at Diya's class? What about your work?" I asked, but Rob ignored me. "Rob?" I asked again. He looked at me, the smile disappearing from his face.

"Can we discuss this later?" he asked.

I looked at Diya, who had already finished her food, and asked her softly, "Diya, if you are finished, do you mind taking Aliya to your bedroom and reading to her for a little while?" Diya nodded her head.

After the girls left, Rob told me he had been let go from his job that afternoon. With the financial markets going down, Rob's firm had decided to shut down the investment fund he had been tasked with launching. They no longer needed him. He gave me the news calmly, waiting for my reaction. I responded calmly to Rob's job loss but with fury at what was happening around us.

All my life I have been a witness to history—especially the history of how a small group of men, using greed and money and power, can control the lives of others. Political and economic systems come and go, but we still haven't been able to think of a system that creates more stability, equality, and sustainability. Why is it so difficult? What—or who—is stopping us?

Channeling my fury, I continued my writing. My writing became my defiant optimism. I found myself in a foreign country teaching graduate students the importance of ground-up social innovation, all while trying to make sense of a financial system meltdown that had hit home—and all this with the challenges of raising two daughters, one with serious health concerns. When everything around me seemed overwhelming, writing about my north star—an inclusive financial system—became the one thing I could control and shape.

I wrote articles about challenging the economic structure and the financial markets. I wrote about which political systems could handle more innovative financial approaches. Each time I published an article, it seemed like I was putting a message in a bottle and setting it afloat in the ocean. Maybe the messages would remain unread, but just writing them helped me find inner strength and hope.

While I hadn't yet fully imagined the specifics, thinking about a more inclusive financial system seemed like the first step toward empowering those who had been left out of the financial system—a system that was now buckling under its own weight.

***

A stock exchange is the pinnacle of financial markets. It is where securities—stocks, bonds, and other financial instruments—are bought and sold. Everything has been traded on stock exchanges: commodities, stocks, bonds, precious metals, and, at its worst, even human beings.

Stock exchanges are designed to connect people who need money for something with people who have money they want to invest. As early as the 1300s, Venetian moneylenders sold loans they had made to their clients to other lenders, thus sowing the seeds of an exchange. Then in the 1500s, in Belgium, people began formally exchanging promissory notes and bonds in a centralized market. But many historians cite as the first true functioning stock exchange the one created to trade shares in the Dutch East India Company in the seventeenth century. To finance the ships that sailed between Europe and Asia to trade spices and other commodities, shipowners needed money to build ships, hire sailors, and buy products. They financed these voyages by selling shares or issuing debt on behalf of "the ship and voyage." These shares and notes were then traded based on news of the ship's progress as it made its way slowly across the oceans. Thus began the rudimentary financial markets, held together by these exchanges. Wealth was created from what men valued as assets and how they perceived risk associated with these assets.

In the more than six hundred years of stock exchanges, however, few had broached the idea of using them to do good. If we could take even a fraction of the trillions of dollars of wealth traded daily on global stock exchanges and point it toward the common good, how much could we accomplish? Now more than ever, as a global crisis darkened our horizon, the world needed financial markets to do things differently.

I had begun to imagine a *social stock exchange*: a trading platform that would connect businesses making positive social and environmental impact with the capital markets and would link a company's financial performance to its social and environmental results. A stock exchange that placed social and environmental returns on equal footing with economic returns would be a game-changer. I had learned how to follow a company's journey and measure its impact. If we could measure the impacts of companies—and then report them, publicly, on a stock exchange—maybe the market would act more humanely.

Creating a social stock exchange—one incorporating quantifiable social and environmental impact and linking businesses that benefit society with investors—would mean taking on the Goliath of the financial world. The slingshot that I would use to take down Goliath was my title: professor. I could speak as a banker or entrepreneur until I was blue in the face without being heard. In Asia, however, a professor is seen as wise and all-knowing. People gave me respect in my role—respect I would wield to the fullest.

"In this sadly crazy historic moment, when every current option is looking bleak and governments are busy cleaning up the private-sector mess, perhaps it is a good time to look some distance into the future toward a gleam of hope for a kinder and gentler form of capitalism," I wrote in an op-ed for the *Daily Star*. "My suggestion is to put together effective regional 'social stock exchanges' in each continent that can spearhead social good through capital markets. I believe Asia is ripe to take the lead in meeting this challenge."

At the time, stock exchanges were often characterized as engines of inequality, existing exclusively of and for the 1 percent. And it's true that the wealthiest 10 percent of Americans owned almost 90 percent of all US stocks. Still, I wasn't sure that stock exchanges were to blame for the wealth inequality they symbolized. As I ruminated on the global financial crisis, I began to wonder whether the fault lay not with the collateralized loan obligations themselves but with how they were used. Similarly, what if stock exchanges themselves were not inherently good or bad but value-neutral? Their power was undeniable. What if we could bend that immense power toward the common good?

***

To be sure, not all was doom and gloom in the financial system. I myself had participated in various ways of using finance for good across the global economy. Microfinance, the practice of providing microloans to poor entrepreneurs to start businesses, demonstrated the power of including the 99 percent in financial markets. Various forms of microfinance had been practiced since Franciscan friars founded community-owned pawnshops in the fifteenth century.

In the 1970s, Ela Bhatt, founder of SEWA (Self-Employed Women's Association) in India, and Muhammad Yunus of Grameen Bank and Sir Fazle Abed of BRAC, both in Bangladesh, pioneered their own unique models of microloans to women entrepreneurs. As I saw through my own work at both Grameen Bank and BRAC, their work created a quiet financial revolution in South Asia. Grameen took this work a step further through its global replication model. With my elementary knowledge of Spanish, I had been part of a training team for South American replicators of the Grameen model and witnessed firsthand how effectively the model could be copied and executed. Professor Yunus's efforts propelled this movement globally, generating infrastructure for microfinance in more than sixty-four countries across the world and spawning a network of organizations that provided capital to these microfinance institutions.

In the United States, SRI, a "do-no-harm" investment methodology, had made headway during the anti-apartheid movement in the 1980s. At Smith, my friends and I urged the university endowment to act as socially responsible investors by refusing to invest in firms that had a negative impact on society and the environment—in our case, South African firms supporting apartheid. With faith-based origins, SRI as a movement initially focused on excluding makers of guns and alcohol and expanded over time to include other "sin" industries. Many mutual funds—funds that raise money from the public to invest in a broad portfolio of securities issued by mostly large companies—began to adopt SRI as a strategy.

Still, doing no harm through investment was not enough to bring about a thoroughgoing change in the financial system. Even at its peak, SRI remained less than 10 percent of the more than $120 trillion in financial markets, and these funds were far removed from the underserved communities and women who were left behind by the financial system. The traditional male-dominated financial institutions and infrastructure still determined the parameters of the system.

Collectively, these pockets of good were pointing finance in the right direction. But I felt these efforts were too little, too exclusive, and too removed from the 99 percent. I needed to find a way to create a whole new financial infrastructure that could value what mattered and in which everyone could be a participant.

Yet it's one thing to write articles and op-eds imagining a social stock exchange; it's another thing to set up a real, functioning one. An entirely new system? Innovative financial products that would value social and environmental impact and give the 99 percent access to capital? Access to quantitative, verifiable impact measurements to guide investors toward companies that were creating social good? A change in investors' perception of risk and return? The whole idea seemed defiant, even audacious. My *Daily Star* article generated interest, and I started receiving emails and speaking invitations, as well as responses suggesting the whole idea was utopian, impossible to achieve. Sometimes even *I* thought it all sounded faintly ridiculous.

Yet another part of me thought: Why not?

CHAPTER TWENTY-FOUR

The Phoenix Rises

As I ran up the narrow path of the hill, the crisp spring air of northern Italy filled my lungs. The path had been artfully carved from a thick forest of oaks, pines, and juniper trees. Pushing against the chilly wind, with the aroma of rosemary bushes that lined the narrow path hanging thick in the air, I finally reached the top. Turning around, I took in the incredible view. There was Lake Como, surrounded by the Italian village of Bellagio. Houses in hues of brown clustered together, holding hundreds of years of history among them. Narrow pathways ran between the houses, all built tightly next to each other, and hundreds of narrow staircases ran in every direction.

I was staying at the historic Villa Serbelloni as a guest of the Bellagio Center of the Rockefeller Foundation, along with nineteen other thought leaders from across the globe. We were discussing how to make finance work for good. Watching the boats crisscrossing the gentle waters, I had to pinch myself to make sure this was real.

When the Rockefeller Foundation wants to embark on something new and innovative to change the world, they tap twenty experts and bring them together for a week in Bellagio. During that time, the group hammers out ideas that can turn into actionable projects. Against the backdrop of the 2008 financial crisis, our gathering would focus on how to galvanize financial markets to do good. The foundation, then headed by Dr. Judith Rodin, a pioneer who had previously broken barriers in the academic world as the first woman President of an Ivy League university, was eager to use their capital to change the financial markets, and they wanted to find out from us how to do it. The twenty participants ranged from heads of stock exchanges to leaders of foundations to entrepreneurs and academics. Our task was clear: to find solutions for rebuilding the financial markets from the ashes of the global financial crisis. We were there to see if we could make a phoenix rise.

I was flattered to be invited but anxious about leaving the girls behind for a whole week. As a woman, I was programmed to always put the needs of others, especially my family, before my own. Many mothers struggle with guilt about pursuing our dreams, and I considered declining the invitation. Rob would not hear of it. "You have to go. Your work, research and writing, all have been leading to this for years," he said adamantly. "I am here. The girls will be fine. This is your opportunity to turn ideas into action! Take it."

So I flew to Milan, where a driver met me at the airport. After an hour-long drive, we entered the cobbled streets of the village, and then there was the gate to the villa. The gate opened, and the sienna-colored villa took my breath away. So many wonderful ideas had germinated in this building. The serene beauty of the villa, the hills, the forest, and the lake all contributed to the enchanting sense of possibility.

The leader of the Rockefeller Foundation delegation was Antony Bugg-Levine, a tall, charismatic, redheaded South African man who took seriously the power bestowed on him by the foundation's billions. Still in a state of shock and jet lag on the first evening, I walked toward our first gathering. Antony approached me, smiling and extending his hand. I looked around. Everyone was holding a cocktail and getting to know each other before the welcome dinner. They all looked so comfortable. Part of me felt like a twenty-one-year-old on her first day on Wall Street. As I scanned the room and noticed that I was the only woman of color there, Antony must have read my mind.

"Don't worry," he said softly. "You'll fit right in with the group, especially wearing that shawl. I can already see how you will make the Western women very jealous." He chuckled a little. He was very direct and clearly had a sense of humor.

"My shawl?" I asked quizzically.

"Yes," he said. "The 'shawl look' is what Western women take on after they visit a developing country. It is their way of saying, 'I have been to the field!'" He grinned conspiratorially. "But you see, you are *from* 'the field.' And you're more qualified than most people here. You'll give them a run for their money!"

He smiled and walked over to greet someone else. I appreciated his words, which helped me get past the pang of imposter syndrome. I took a deep breath. As a woman from the Global South, with qualifications from both Wall Street and the last mile, I realized anew my status as both insider and outsider. And I wondered if shaking up the financial system might be easier for someone who had never fully belonged to it in the first place.

***

Breaking up into groups across the various rooms in the villa, we spent hours together over the next three days, hashing out the important elements of a new form of finance and investing. What would it take to change finance to do good? What does it even mean to invest for good? How should we define it, and what should this new way of investing be called?

During this discovery process, Antony introduced the term *impact investing* as a possible way to describe what we were talking about. The term caught on, and we began using it in our discussions. We talked about how to establish the practice of impact investing, how to introduce impact measurement into investing decisions, which stakeholders needed to be involved and how to ensure they would have a voice in the process. These were the same questions I had been addressing with my research, writing, and teaching. Discussing these concepts with influential people from around the world—people who had been on similar intellectual journeys—was thrilling.

One afternoon, as we were debating and brainstorming and drawing diagrams on whiteboards, I began to worry that we were running out of time. I wondered whether we'd leave Bellagio without having decided what financial infrastructure would spur the growth of this new impact investing market. "We need to address the elephant in the room," I blurted out to my group in exasperation. They sat there silently, ready to listen. I began an impassioned speech to my small audience.

"To change the system, we need to build a platform to bring together many different constituents," I said. "We need to create social stock exchanges as a beacon to attract enterprises that are doing good and as an investment marketplace where they can raise capital to grow. These exchanges will validate positive impact alongside financial outcomes so that investors can factor this positive impact into their investment decisions. These exchanges would then pull together investors and other stakeholders to make capital move. So it's a top-down, bottom-up approach."

I was in my element. Over the next few days, our discussions turned toward how a social stock exchange would work. I loved ideating with heads of financial institutions and making a case for creating a new highway of financing for hope. Creating a social stock exchange that could include the 99 percent wouldn't be easy. But we hadn't been assembled at Bellagio to do things that were easy, or in the way they had always been done; we were there to dream a new way of doing finance into existence.

***

The last morning was a flurry of goodbyes. My flight was leaving in the afternoon, so I waited downstairs and chatted with new friends as they gathered their bags to leave. I was standing at the entrance of the villa when Antony walked over.

"Durreen, do you have a minute?" he asked in a serious voice. His expression concerned me, and I wondered if I had said something wrong during the last meeting or if something had happened to Rob or the kids. We walked out to the garden and stood by the rosemary bushes, with a full view of the lake in front of us.

"I want you to start something." Antony said.

"What do you mean?" I had no idea what he was talking about.

"My colleagues at the foundation and I have heard what you had to say over the last few days," he continued. "We have read your work, and we have now seen your passion. We can see that you have it in you to change the financial system for good. We want you to become an entrepreneur again."

Antony was smiling now. "We will support anything you want to do, be it starting a social enterprise, creating a social stock exchange, or launching an impact investment fund. Anything."

I hadn't been expecting this. It's one thing to talk about changing the world. But when a foundation director tells you he will support your idea for doing so: well, I was starting to feel dizzy. All my life I had craved respect and longed for people to believe in me. I had worked so hard to try and fit in. I had heard the word "no" so often as a little girl in Dhaka and then again as a woman pitching to Silicon Valley investors. Now, at long last, I had a "yes"—and I didn't know what to do.

Then again, I *did* know. If I accepted his offer, I'd work to create a financial system that put women, underserved communities, and the environment at the very center. I would create something that my daughters would be proud to say their mother had made.

So I thanked Antony and told him I would do it. Antony exhaled and smiled. "Write the business plan, and tell me how much funding you will need to make it a reality. I look forward to hearing from you. Now let's go and catch our planes." With that, Antony hurried back to the villa to pick up his suitcase.

I stood there next to the pine tree, stunned, taking in the smell of pine and rosemary and wondering what had just happened. And what in the world would happen next.

PART V

Create Your Own Change

CHAPTER TWENTY-FIVE

Put One Foot in Front of the Other

"Girls, walk close to the wall—and stay away from the edge of the staircase!" I whispered, hopefully loudly enough to be heard not only by my daughters but also by the man showing us around the garment factory. "I can't believe there is no railing! Be very careful and look down, because the cement is crumbling on some of the stairs. And stay away from the exposed wires!"

I looked back past Diya and Aliya and glared at our guide, the manager of a garment factory in Dhaka, Bangladesh. He needed to hear that his employees were working in a death trap. Climbing up the stairs carefully, I kept thinking of the hundreds of women who worked here. Every day they had to walk up and down this treacherous staircase, past exposed wires hanging from the wall. Two red tin buckets filled with sand and labeled *agoon* (fire) in white paint sat on the floor. Apparently, workers were expected to use sand from these two small buckets to put out any fires that might occur in this massive building full of flammable materials.

We reached the third floor, where hundreds of women hunched over rows of sewing machines while a handful of men cut fabric using electric blade machinery on a steel table. In one corner, a group of women inspected the completed garments for quality control. I picked up a pair of red-lace panties from the piles of clothing ready for packaging. Toiling in a hazard-ridden factory in Dhaka, these women were making lingerie for women in the West with no idea of the end use of the piece of garment.

Looking across the cavernous room, I saw women wearing colorful cotton saris, their heads covered, working away, row after row, bent over the sewing machines. They were singularly focused on meeting their output targets. Just like the village women I had worked with at Grameen Bank, these women were the backbone of the country. They worked hard for a living and to lift themselves and their families out of poverty. By doing this work, they were optimistically embracing economic opportunity while defying the patriarchy. Like American women during World War II, they had emerged from their homes to join the formal economy.

Dhaka was one stop on a tour for my university research, which focused on how to measure the impact of a company's operations on its employees and other stakeholders. It was 2009, and Bangladesh had replaced China as the garment-manufacturing center for the West. The women of this country were toiling to ensure the fast fashion shelves of GAP, H&M, Old Navy, Target, and Zara were fully stocked. Yes, these women were earning money for the first time, just like women who received loans from Grameen Bank. In this case, however, they were not running their own businesses. They were working for newly minted businessmen who were taking their cues from the West. And the message these businessmen heard was this: all that matters are operational efficiency and bringing down costs for Western buyers.

The garment industry was responsible for 80 percent of Bangladesh's total exports, with the United States being the biggest market. Bengal (the historical name of Bangladesh and the North East region of India, predating British rule) had been the textile hub of Asia since the sixteenth century, producing muslin and cotton and serving as a trade route for silk from China. Over the centuries, the importance of the sector had ebbed and flowed. In the 1980s, the newly industrialized Asian countries of Korea, Hong Kong, Taiwan, and China started using Bangladesh as part of their production chain for cheaper labor. Over the following decades, with government assistance, the industry had grown and become the largest primary supplier to the market.

So in a way, these women at their sewing machines were playing their part in the war against poverty. And these jobs did allow them to increase their families' income. Yet there's a fine line between giving someone an opportunity and exploiting them. Throughout history, economic growth for one group has often occurred via the exploitation of another group, be it women, the poor, Black people, or any other vulnerable group. That pattern of exploitation extends to abuse of the environment as well: the extraction of resources that damages the voiceless earth and its ecosystems for financial gain.

Financial markets need frameworks for measurement. To be effective, these frameworks must link to risk and return, which in turn determine the right amount of capital, at the right price, for each use case.

So while the growth of the garment sector allowed thousands of Bangladeshi women to earn a livelihood for the first time, I still wondered: how much were these new job opportunities turning into abuse? Were the women's voices and needs being heard? I needed to see it all firsthand, so I organized a research trip to focus on new small and growing Asian businesses.

On the factory tour, my girls were busy making friends with the women and generally making themselves at home. Deep in the sewing lines, Diya and Aliya, in their halting Bengali, asked the women question after question: "How do you get the stitches just right? How many of these shirts can you finish in a day? What's your favorite design?" I saw the smiles of amusement on the women's faces. They proudly showed the girls the designs they were making and let them touch the machines and inspect the pieces of cloth.

Soon Diya came back to where our guide and I were standing. "Uncle, could I use the bathroom? I can use the bathroom the working aunties use," she asked. Diya addressed him and the women workers respectfully, as we address elders in my culture: Uncle and Aunty.

The manager's face fell, an expression of discomfort washing over him. "Well, little girl, the bathrooms are downstairs. When we go downstairs, you can use it," he said.

"But, Uncle, that is a really dangerous staircase. The aunties need to go up and down these stairs just to use the bathroom?" Diya pressed. I smiled to myself, imagining her future as a lawyer.

"Well, they don't need to go up and down several times, because they go to the bathroom only when they get bathroom breaks," our guide explained. "If you let them go to the bathroom whenever they want, they won't be able to finish the work."

This answer was not satisfactory for Diya. "But at school we can go to the bathroom whenever we need to. What's the difference? Also, the stairs are so dangerous. You said they have bathroom breaks. But what if someone falls when they go down in big groups during their breaks?"

By this point, sweat was rolling down the man's face, and he was clearly looking for a way to end this tour. He ignored Diya and looked at me. "Madam, if we are done here, maybe we can go to Sir's office?"

***

Back in the management office, I started asking the CEO questions about the women's working conditions: their hours, wages, and opportunities to express grievances. I wanted to know how much the women's voices and well-being factored into the company's operations. Then I pushed on the blatant safety violations we had seen all around the building.

At this point, the CEO lost his cool. "You are a professor and not a journalist, so I can tell you this," he said. "I am an entrepreneur. I am running a business, and I need to pay my bills. I'm providing jobs for these women, who were basically sitting at home before this. I am giving them meals, transportation, a bonus on Eid, and paid leave."

He took a breath and continued. "Can I do more? Yes—but only if I can charge the buyers more! The T-shirt I am selling for two dollars to a Western retail giant gets sold for fifteen. If that retailer tried to charge twenty-five dollars for that T-shirt, would people buy it? No. If I charged the retailer five dollars for the T-shirt and used the extra money to help the women, would the retailer buy from me? No. They would go to another factory that was selling it for two. So tell me: What do you want me to do?"

The owner was clearly frustrated, and I had some sympathy for him. I knew all too well how hard it is to be an entrepreneur. Running a company while managing the impact of that company is not easy. I had done it once, and I was gearing up to do it again now. While I continued teaching at the university, I had also begun writing the business plan for a new company, Impact Investment Exchange (IIX), with the prospect of support from the Rockefeller Foundation.

Already, through my research, my team had developed and begun using a novel methodology that assigned value to the positive impact that companies created in the real economy. Using this methodology, my company would help innovative impact enterprises raise money from the financial system to support and grow their impact.

In writing the business plan, my team of volunteers and friends and I were learning about financial innovation and social entrepreneurship in real time. And my daughters had become my research assistants, tagging along with me on visits to garment factories in Bangladesh, environmentally friendly coffee producers in Thailand, and sustainable fish processors in Indonesia. School holidays became journeys of discovery in places their friends never even knew existed. In our travels, I sought out companies that IIX could eventually support and help grow. These were companies granting as much importance to creating a positive impact for women, society, and the environment as they were to profitability and growth.

Sitting in the factory office now, I watched a fellow entrepreneur performing his own balancing act between profit and the well-being of his employees.

"When I began construction on this factory, I counted on a bank loan, but it never came through," he explained. "So as you saw, the factory looks like a half-made, dilapidated building. I could not finish building without the loan! Will the bank give me a loan for treating the women well? No!"

His frustration boiled over into anger, and I was glad the girls were outside walking around, checking out the showrooms. "I understand your frustration. Believe me, I do," I told him. "I'm an entrepreneur myself. I know how hard it is to start and run a business. This question—whether banks will lend us money for doing good—is exactly what I'm trying to help us all answer. I am trying to measure the positive and negative impact of a company's activities. If we can do that, then maybe you could get rewarded for doing the right thing by getting cheaper loans."

Seeing the man's anger defuse a bit, I smiled and continued. "Because you're right: the system needs to be changed. We need to create a system where every stakeholder understands his or her responsibility in it and acts accordingly. I am hoping my research helps address this problem. My goal is to get the right kind of capital for you that will reward you for treating your employees fairly."

With that, I got up and bid him goodbye, realizing anew the enormity of the task on which I had embarked.

The social justice issues relating to the treatment of garment workers were pretty evident as they were right in front of us. In a country like Bangladesh, however, environmental harm created by the garment sector was also taking place on a massive scale. The rivers were polluted with dyes, because no regulations around dumping of chemicals existed. Companies often dumped chemicals into the same rivers from which people drank water.

The global rise in temperature meant sea levels were rising, and Bangladesh, a river delta just a few feet above sea level, was losing land to the rising sea. Even my mother's ancestral home was now under water. With the loss of land and drastic change in climate, many farming families looking to save their lot were sacrificing their daughters by selling them off to traffickers or marrying them off as children. Girls needed to walk miles to get water or firewood, journeys during which their safety was often endangered.

People and the planet were intertwined. We could not save one without the other. We needed to measure the impact and value of both in the financial markets.

***

Once again, I was an entrepreneur, but this time, I was not just creating a company; I was building a new financial system. Graduating from being an entrepreneur who builds a business to becoming a *systemapreneur*—someone who builds an entire ecosystem—seemed daunting. And my life had become a mix of overlapping responsibilities with few boundaries. My daughters, my students, my friends, and my work: all were intertwined. I was teaching, researching, and now starting a company, all while raising a family that included a child with special needs. Aliya was now four years old, and I was still waking up several times a night to care for her skin. In the middle of the night, fighting sleep, I would quietly spray her body and massage her with medicated lotions.

And my experience with Aliya was spilling into everything I was doing intellectually. How do you integrate someone into a society that wants to reject them? Why does society reject certain people? I would think about Diya, a little girl who was witnessing and at times being pulled into fighting battles for her sister. She represented the people in society who want to make systems more inclusive for those they love. They may be on the sidelines, but they can be an important part of creating change. How could we empower the Diyas of the world to bring about change?

Caring for Aliya taught me to break life into little pieces to survive. When something is huge and beyond your control, you start living for the small moments. You break up the enormity into manageable pieces and focus on those small, tiny battles. Winning small victories—like watching Aliya's happiness in the bathtub—gave me so much energy. In those times, the enormous tasks that lay ahead somehow didn't seem so overwhelming or impossible.

The battle ahead of us—for our family and for the larger world of financial markets—was not about getting Aliya to fit into a system or empowering Diya to be an ally or fighter on her sister's behalf. The work before us was about creating a system that would naturally make room for both of them.

CHAPTER TWENTY-SIX

Invest in Women

Iblinked several times and then squinted to adjust to the bright sun. Women in saris were riding motorbikes all around me. Was I dreaming? The dusty road, the gentle sway of the bamboo cart drawn by bullocks, the creaky noise of the wheels, and the warm afternoon sun: all were having a soporific effect. Sitting precariously on the flat bamboo plaque of the cart, I rested my dupatta-covered head on my knees, which were tightly drawn up to my chest.

A motorbike zoomed by, and a woman's voice barked to the bullock-cart driver in Tamil, the local language. I jerked my head up and watched in awe as she passed us. She was obviously in a hurry and not happy that our slow, steer-drawn cart was blocking the narrow unpaved road.

Savita, a doctoral student and my research assistant, and I were on our way to the village center a few hours away from the bustling downtown of Chennai, a major city in South India. This was another stop on my hunt for undervalued companies creating a positive impact. I needed good case studies for my academic research, and financially sustainable companies creating a positive impact would demonstrate the importance of social return. Today we'd visit a village center of the Bullock Cart Workers Development Association (BWDA), which disseminates loans to women-owned businesses.

"Savita, is the heat getting to me, or was that a woman in a sari riding a motorbike?"

Savita, who had grown up in Chennai, laughed in her soft, polite way. "Prof, you are in South India. Women here are much more empowered than in the rest of South Asia. This is a matriarchal society, so women's leadership and women's empowerment are part of everyday life."

Savita was right. Chennai seemed worlds apart culturally from my life in Bangladesh. In fact, this was why I wanted to study South India. Women here were more educated and better integrated into the economy than women in the other parts of the Indian subcontinent. I wanted to see this dynamic with my own eyes.

While BWDA had started as a support organization for bullock-cart drivers, its membership grew rapidly when it began including the drivers' female family members. BWDA's founder was Dr. Joslin Thambi. He was the son of a bullock-cart worker and drove a bullock cart himself to pay for his college education. Even though there were nearly 30 million bullock-cart workers in India, they lacked a social safety net. As members of low social strata, bullock-cart workers were often abused by police and cheated out of fares.

In 1985, Dr. Thambi secured some grant funding to start BWDA. His vision was to provide a forum for workers to organize and represent themselves to the Indian government. He also wanted BWDA to contribute to the overall welfare of workers and their families. A BWDA study in the state of Tamil Nadu concluded that most workers' families were at the mercy of extractive local moneylenders for emergency funds.

To counter this, BWDA began forming self-help or lender groups among its workers' family members. These groups encouraged members to save regularly and thereby create a shared pool of savings. Pooled savings were then shared among the group on a rotating basis through internal loans, eventually reducing members' dependence on moneylenders.

Around that time, in the mid-1980s, women became a big part of BWDA's membership, spurring the organization's growth. The

BWDA that we were now working with had nearly half a million clients, mostly women, and its loans to members amounted to many millions of dollars.

Walking around the villages of Tamil Nadu, Savita and I watched women speeding by us on motorbikes. We visited women business owners as they ran small grocery stores, tailor shops, and beauty parlors. Economic growth was happening in front of our eyes! This is how a whole village grows: when women receive capital to create and grow businesses. The convergence of a matriarchal society, public policy intervention, and organizations like BWDA had resulted in economic flourishing. My heart swelled as I thought of what happens when women get the right opportunity.

To keep this women-powered engine of growth going, BWDA needed a continuous influx of money from larger financial markets to lend to its members. As expected, however, financial markets did not place any value on the positive impact of BWDA's operations, making it hard for BWDA to raise capital and reach more women.

After meeting with us to discuss the details of his business operation and its impact on the community, I watched Dr. Thambi meet with financial institutions from Mumbai, the finance capital of India. Each time, after a thorough review, the bank representatives complimented BWDA's operations, dedicated staff, and loyal clientele. Yet in the same breath, they suggested that Dr. Thambi increase the interest rate that BWDA charged clients. From the bankers' perspective, it was a logical suggestion. Raising rates would bring BWDA's rates closer to those charged by other lenders in India. And why wouldn't BWDA want to maximize its profits?

Dr. Thambi explained to them that BWDA was very different from other organizations they had in mind. BWDA's social mission—improving the welfare of its members—was not mere lip service. It was BWDA's raison d'être. Keeping its interest rates affordable for its poorest members was a key part of delivering on this mission.

The frustrating conversations sounded all too familiar. My mind flashed to the venture capital firms pressuring oneNest to change our business model. Banks and investors would pat mission-driven entrepreneurs on the back, tell them they were doing a great job, and then walk away without providing them the capital they needed. Seeing this pattern on my research tour fueled the fire inside me: to create a company that would support the BWDAs and oneNests of the world.

***

The white marble building and gently swaying bamboo kept the relentless sun at bay. The air felt almost comfortable, a rare occurrence in the humid climate of Singapore. I was sitting with a small group of volunteers and former students, hashing out the nuances of the business plan for our new company in one of the university's century-old British colonial-style buildings.

Among the group was Rob, whom I had recently convinced to join Impact Investment Exchange. We needed people with a strong finance background on the IIX team. We needed to build our own investment platforms and maybe even new types of investments. Creating an entire impact investing ecosystem would require people with expertise like Rob's. The job offer I had made him included an irresistible salary package of zero dollars. But he had accepted the new role, which also included the chance to reinvent finance to do good for millions.

If Grameen Bank was the bank for the poor, we wanted to become the investment bank for companies that benefit the poor. IIX would use financial know-how to structure the deals and apply our proprietary methodology to measure the impact of the company's operation on women's lives, families, and communities.

Together our group mulled over the business plan, reading sections aloud, working and reworking the core ideas. We asked ourselves questions to make our plan airtight. Who would the stock exchange benefit? Our answer: women, underserved communities, and the environment. How? By bringing all these stakeholders into the financial system. Beyond dollars, the stock exchange would place a value on the voice and participation of each of these stakeholders.

Why a social stock exchange? Frankly, symbolism was one compelling reason. If we could create a stock exchange for high-impact enterprises, impact investment could take its place on the global stage.

We knew the success of the stock exchange depended on creating an ecosystem to support it. Companies don't just happen to get listed on a stock exchange; they require coaching, strategy, and development before they become investable enough for the open market. I had seen firsthand on Wall Street how the traditional financial system grooms companies for the stock exchange by emphasizing profit above all else. In creating a social stock exchange, we had to create our own way to groom companies: by emphasizing profits and positive impact together, not at the expense of one another. We had to create an entire ecosystem of investors and supporting activities oriented around impact. Building this system would require us to educate both investors and enterprises. Above all else, it would require new ways of measuring impact.

We also needed to make a case for Singapore. Why would we base the company here? I looked at the group, trusting their wisdom and analysis. "Well, it is rapidly becoming the financial hub for Asia," Rob suggested. "Especially after Hong Kong was handed back to China, investors and financial institutions are flocking to Singapore's stable and clean financial infrastructure."

My friend Sue, who had just moved to Singapore from New York, added that we could capitalize on the Singapore government's aim to become the "Switzerland" of Asia by attracting private wealth managers and their clients from Asia and beyond.

"Prof, this is exactly what we have been talking about in class—the newly unequal distribution of wealth in Asia!" my student Will chimed in, with his usual enthusiasm. "How can we use the financial market to redistribute this wealth? Through stakeholder capitalism—or, as you call it, conscious capitalism," another student Sikander added with his usual seriousness. I smiled. The can-do spirit of young people invigorated the rest of us. It felt like we were piecing together a manifesto for a revolution—a revolution to make the financial system do good.

Before long I had submitted the business plan to the Rockefeller Foundation, and they delivered on their promise to financially support my vision. Armed with a plan and seed funding, we now faced the great unknown. I did not know the direction this path would take, but I trusted my team with all my heart and believed in the beauty of the idea. That was enough to get started.

***

The key to any successful marketplace is to bring together as many buyers and sellers as possible in one place to make it easy for them to transact. Companies like Amazon and eBay spend millions of dollars to acquire customers and encourage these transactions. We did not have the resources to spend lavishly to bring together buyers and sellers. So we reached out initially to a few hundred enterprises and investors from our networks, including high-impact enterprises I had encountered during my research. We invited them to join our newly minted Impact Partners platform: an online exchange connecting impact enterprises and impact investors.

Slowly but surely, Impact Partners began attracting high-impact enterprises seeking money to fund their growth. Investors were beginning to peruse these enterprises on our online platform, but actual transactions were not yet taking place. I knew that transactions would not just happen without active encouragement. These enterprises were seeking to raise hundreds of thousands of dollars or more. The investors we had assembled had the capacity to provide this, but they needed more information to make investment decisions. We needed to bring the enterprises and investors closer together, greasing the wheels like investment bankers do for companies in the traditional financial markets.

One of the first companies we had picked to be listed on the exchange was BagoSphere. Its founder, Zhihan Lee, was a soft-spoken Singaporean man in his early twenties with an engineering degree who had moved to the Philippines to train the youth and especially women from underserved communities in basic technology skills and call center work. Zhihan had founded Bago-Sphere with a clear social mission: to increase the income of its trainees by preparing them for good-paying jobs without requiring them to leave their home areas and migrate to the overcrowded capital region. To raise money from impact investors, BagoSphere would need to communicate this impact clearly to investors while also demonstrating two things. First, it needed to show that it was able to earn revenue and make profits. Second, BagoSphere had to prove that an equity infusion—money invested in return for a share of the company—could help the company grow and serve more trainees while earning more income. In return, the investors could benefit from the growth of the company as the value of the company increased over time.

BagoSphere charged its students a nominal upfront tuition fee. The students would pay off the balance of the fee only once they found jobs. BagoSphere also set up channels to help place them in jobs, ensuring that women would be employed after they completed the training. This strategy would also ensure the company's tuition loans were being paid off.

Through our impact assessment, we needed to make sure that the training and the jobs that BagoSphere provided were making a real difference in women's lives and having a ripple effect of positive impact on their families and communities. Any kind of "loan" to the vulnerable can be tricky, as you must ensure that the payment terms are fair and that those who can't repay are treated with respect. In this case, everything checked out, and we were ready to make a big splash with this company.

I was thrilled that the company was from the Philippines, my second home. Despite a more than 90 percent literacy rate and the People Power revolution I had witnessed, the country still suffered from structural economic issues. A small group of rich families still owned most of the country's land and wealth.

Zhihan told me stories of women that brought tears to my eyes. He spoke of twenty-four-year-old Shena, who had recounted to Zhihan the hardships that brought her to BagoSphere. As a teenager, Shena had worked as a domestic helper to support her nine siblings. Even after she got married, life did not get any better as her husband, a sugarcane plantation worker, barely could scrape together enough income to feed themselves and their two children. When the family's only asset, a buffalo, died, Shena's mother-in-law encouraged her to enroll in BagoSphere's call center training. Shena was nervous because she had completed only a few years of schooling and even then had not done well academically.

But Shena did not quit. After several months of training and a few rejections, she landed a job at a call center and worked hard. As soon as she saved some money, Shena bought a motorcycle for her husband and began saving again to buy a new buffalo. Economic independence brought Shena a whole new level of hope and confidence. And Shena's story gave Zhihan the strong desire to grow the company and train hundreds more women like her.

After weeks of coaching and support from the IIX team, Zhihan made his pitch in front of a group of Impact Partners' investors who had registered interest on the investment platform. With help from Rob and the rest of the Impact Partners team, Zhihan was ready with his business plan and impact assessment. He presented his growth plans and impact story and explained how BagoSphere would utilize the $120,000 investment it was seeking to progress to the next stage. Our impact measurement framework clearly demonstrated the positive impact of the training on each woman and the ripple effect on her family and the community. With a social return on investment of more than $3 for every dollar invested, BagoSphere proved an attractive social investment proposition. We had successfully shown that the impact created by a company can be measured and that it can go hand in hand with expectations of financial return.

Over the next few weeks, investors rallied around Zhihan's vision, and we celebrated closing the first deal on the Impact Partners platform. The first social stock exchange in the world was in action!

***

The social stock exchange we created was what the finance world called a private placement platform. Within a handful of years we turned the platform into the world's largest private placement platform dedicated to impact investment. A private placement platform enables companies to issue securities that are sold to a small group of investors as a means of raising capital. While the platform didn't yet allow investors to trade shares among themselves, it did enable companies with a strong positive social and environmental impact to raise money from investors.

Unlocking hundreds of millions of dollars for positive impact is not for the faint of heart. On the investor side, we had to confront a lack of understanding of impact investing and overcome deep biases. These were the same investors who blithely wrote checks for philanthropy projects—for which they had no idea whether their money would create the desired impact—and who invested millions in dubious technologies pitched to them by people who looked like them. When it came to investing in impact enterprises, however, these investors became doubly cautious, focusing on the financial returns first and impact second, and scrutinizing both. They made unreasonable demands around financial returns from the investment—and also insisted that the venture create impact that was deeper than that of their usual philanthropic endeavors! These investors truly wanted to have their cake and eat it too. We had our impact measurement framework, but we clearly had more work to do to convince conventional investors to start seeing differently what it means to have triple bottom line returns: financial, social, and environmental.

Traditional investors perceived our impact enterprises as "risky" investments because of the companies' commitment to social good rather than pure profit. In order to demystify the notion of "risk" from investing in impact enterprises, we needed to ensure there were stakeholders along the way to help them grow. We had to continuously educate and engage new players, nurturing not only the impact enterprises but the supportive ecosystem as well. In the process, we had to earn enough money to pay our bills, spread the word, keep the momentum going, and most importantly, make sure that the women in the last mile were becoming a part of the financial system.

Our young team members loved doing fieldwork, which included traveling to the remote countryside where the enterprises we supported had their operations. They traveled to smallholder rice producers in Cambodia, a water filtration facility on the island of Sumatra, a cashew processing facility in Bali, Indonesia, and clean energy producers in Uttar Pradesh, India. Doing our due diligence meant measuring the operational and financial aspects of these enterprises, as well as their social and environmental impacts. We would then present that data on the Impact Partners platform, where investors could view it and evaluate each investment opportunity.

Following our success with BagoSphere, our team got to work raising capital for a wide range of other impact enterprises. Among the early companies for which we helped find expansion capital were a healthcare company providing low-cost eye care, including surgery, in mobile clinics on a "pay what you can" basis in the hills of Assam, India; a peer-to-peer energy-sharing company in Bangladesh that allowed villagers to sell energy generated by solar home systems to their neighbors; and an organic coconut sugar producer raising the income of smallholder farmers in Indonesia.

We began accumulating wins, which were rewarding. But we still felt like we were boiling the ocean in terms of building an entire ecosystem to support the growth of the impact investment market—while at the same time ensuring that IIX itself was financially sustainable. Although we were now operating a successful private placement platform, I still wanted to create a public social stock exchange. A public exchange, with the proper regulations, could help impact enterprises raise even larger amounts of capital to connect women from underserved communities to powerful global financial markets. It could bring much-needed and widespread legitimacy to businesses operating with a purpose.

That opportunity came the day I received an email from Tamzin, whom I'd met at the Bellagio gathering. Tamzin had founded Nexii, a company developing a public social stock exchange with the

Mauritius government. She had made a lot of progress but didn't have the steam to continue, and she wanted IIX to take over her company to bring the work to fruition. Within weeks we had drafted the legal documents with the pro bono help of a law firm. Tamzin wrote the press release about the acquisition and set the tone for the narrative. She was a visionary in her own right, and I wanted to make sure she had a good closure with her company.

As soon as Nexii was part of IIX, our general counsel Matt brought in another large US law firm who volunteered to work pro bono on finalizing the regulatory work for the social stock exchange. Thus we began the work of creating a public stock exchange.

Dipping our toes into the big ocean of financial markets meant relying on the kindness of others, especially law firms that provided their services for free. So many partners came forward to help us build IIX and the ecosystem. Changing a system for the good of humanity and the planet means being inclusive and inviting others into your tent. The tent may be crowded, and people in it may have strong opinions, but we held in common the goal that every discussion and action led toward an inclusive financial system. The zero-sum capitalist approach had created the system of haves and have-nots that we were struggling against—a system in which some people win at the expense of others and nobody wants to share. As we built a new system from the ground up, we were determined to do so on the sturdy foundation of generosity, trust, and inclusion.

CHAPTER TWENTY-SEVEN

Find Strength in Friends and Allies

As years passed and IIX grew, we needed to raise more capital so that we could create the right kind of infrastructure for this inclusive financial system. The seed funding from the Rockefeller Foundation had gone to good use getting IIX this far, but we needed additional capital to keep growing. The irony was clear: even as we were bringing investment capital to grow impact enterprises, we had not been able to get anyone to invest in IIX. What we were doing was too risky, too revolutionary, too "women-focused." It felt like a situation of the cobbler's children not having shoes. And it took me back to my oneNest days: knowing in my core that we could build an equitable world but struggling to convince others that it would work.

Scrounging around for funding, I gave endless talks and took countless meetings. I was willing to speak at any conference that even remotely touched on sustainability or had wealthy people in attendance. Crisscrossing Asia, Europe, and the United States, I was spreading the gospel of making finance do good for the 99 percent.

A few years earlier I had spoken at the TED conference in Los Angeles. Wearing a red sari I had bought with my mother, I had made the case in my TED Talk for a financial system that delivered on its promise of providing prosperity for all. I said a lot of things in that talk—about defiant optimism and about using capital for good.

But the sari I wore probably spoke as loudly as I did. My sari represented the creative labor and entrepreneurial spirit of women in underserved communities. They were the drivers of the new system we were building. It was dyed to a brick red with vegetable dye, a traditional, environmentally sustainable method revived by women from a weaving cooperative. They had stitched the fabric with nakshi stitches and motifs, those designs I'd watched my grandmother and the women in Bangladeshi villages create.

I remember how much Ma had loved the sari. We had both marveled at the thousands of tiny stitches on the five yards of silk, thinking of the hundreds of hours of meticulous work that had made the sari possible. That day when I spoke at the TED conference, I felt like the sari was giving me strength: from Ma, who always supported women and small enterprises, and from the women we were working with all over the world.

The TED gathering had been a massive production. Attendees included the superrich and the ultrarich, the famous and the spectacularly famous, from Wall Street, Silicon Valley, and Hollywood: Bill Gates, Jeff Bezos, Al Gore, Will Smith, and so on. Tickets started at $8,000. Nearly a thousand people attended in person and by video from other locations. As excited as I felt to be there, I couldn't get past how odd it was that such a spectacular event, held for the common good, was filled with people who were unreachable by common people.

In the span of four days, I spoke to founder of Amazon Jeff Bezos, founder of LinkedIn Reid Hoffman, and many other luminaries. But a sari-clad woman talking about taking down a system that had so richly benefited them? It did not hold appeal for most. The rich and powerful have their own idea of what they want the world to look like. While a gathering like TED exposed them to "new ideas," they tended to accept only those ideas that reinforced their position at the top of the pyramid. Who wants to rock a system that advantages you and your friends?

But I kept showing up at conferences, talking about IIX and the highway we were building between investors and impact enterprises.

So when I received an invitation to speak on a panel at the Wharton School of the University of Pennsylvania, alongside big-wigs from high-powered investment firms, I jumped at the chance.

***

As I expected, at the Wharton gathering I was the only sari-clad woman in a sea of suits. Women had comprised less than 20 percent of the student population at Wharton when I was a student, and this alumni gathering reflected that ratio. Finance clearly remained a man's world.

I said hello to a few familiar faces at the conference. Jeff Sheehan, the associate dean of international relations at Wharton who had invited me, was an ally and one of many people quietly playing a role in the movement. The panel that he had put together, "Creative Solutions to Investing Challenges," gave me the chance to make my case—that finance can work in a more equitable way—to a room full of financial titans.

The discussion started by focusing on various innovative financial products and solutions. Soon, however, I started pushing on the *why* and the *who*. Why are we creating these innovative solutions? And who benefits from them? It's possible to make finance more inclusive, I said, giving examples from our work.

The other three panelists were men wearing expensive dark suits. They very effectively represented the concerns of the rich and powerful 1 percent—frankly, probably the .01 percent. As I spoke, they started to shift in their chairs and shake their heads. Their discomfort was palpable, but I ignored it. By this point in my career, I enjoyed the discomfort of the privileged. Discomfort often comes from the realization that one is doing something wrong.

As I spoke, an entire volcano of discomfort erupted. One of the panelists, who headed up a large investment fund, got visibly upset. His face flushed, and he started interrupting and speaking over me. With a loud voice clearly intended to shut me down, he said, "My job is to maximize my clients' ROI (return on investment). I can't be bothered with evaluating the businesses on any criterion except maximum income and growth! I could not, in good conscience, recommend an investment that I knew might have a lower return just because it was socially worthy." He concluded with a chuckle of disbelief.

Before I could collect myself, one of the Wharton School board members, Matt Green, stood up. One of a handful of Black financial leaders on Wall Street, Matt had an authoritative manner and could command the attention of the entire room. "I think that is a very myopic way of looking at finance," he said calmly, looking around the room. "What Durreen is saying here is not to abandon growth but to make it inclusive. We all, as Wharton alums, have the responsibility to use the fantastic degrees we've earned to look at finance more holistically. As Durreen said, it's not about lowering returns. It's about maximizing a *combined* return: financial and social."

At these words, the whole room broke out in applause. The man on the panel who made the comment looked annoyed. But he did not have a chance for a rebuttal as Jeff wrapped up the panel and people in the audience approached me to hear more.

As with any attempt to overcome barriers and make the world more just and equitable, having allies makes all the difference.

***

Not long after the Wharton panel, I spent a morning meeting with venture capitalists in Silicon Valley. Everyone politely made clear that IIX's business model was not even close to anything their firm would support. The experience reminded me of when I had first visited Silicon Valley to raise capital for oneNest. By this time, I was used to hearing no, and I no longer took it to heart.

My last meeting of the day was with an Indian American venture capitalist I had met at the TED conference. He had introduced himself as a Silicon Valley veteran and founder of one of the largest enterprise software companies. At the time, he struck me as arrogant and condescending, questioning my theories and claiming to know all there is to know about financial markets and developing economies. (And here I thought he was a software engineer!) But I was used to this treatment, especially from men from my part of the world, so I tried to remain optimistic that this last meeting might unlock the investment IIX needed.

At my side was Kalpana Raina, a retired Wall Street banker I had met at an Asia Society gathering and with whom I had forged a bond of mentor and mentee. She had offered to help me enlist the support of venture capital firms. So there we were, Kalpana and I, sitting in the waiting area of a well-known fund run by a billionaire. The decor of the sitting area—beige, modern, but cold—matched the mood inside the building. Here in Palo Alto, the arid home of venture capitalism, the architecture mirrored the tech industry's values: efficiency and profit maximization. A beautiful receptionist in a very low-cut, body-fitting blouse and skirt emerged to greet us. She looked just like all the other support staff who had walked past as we waited: all women, all pretty, all young, generously proportioned, and wearing tight, revealing clothes. Kalpana and I exchanged glances. "Well, I hope it gets better," I whispered, as one of the women ushered us into a conference room.

Before long, a tall lean Indian man, clad in a black turtleneck and expensive designer jeans à la Steve Jobs, walked in. We greeted each other, and before long the conversation turned into the second round of condescension, picking up where he had left off at TED.

He was an impact investor himself, he claimed. But it was clear that our definitions of the term were very different. Even as I tried to explain the value of investing in women, I knew I was wasting my breath. Employing only women willing to look and dress like Barbie suggested he had a different view of women than we did.

As I had experienced many times before with powerful men, the "conversation" quickly turned into humiliation and repudiation when we apparently did not adequately acknowledge his wisdom. Kalpana tried to jump in a few times to bring the conversation back to IIX's accomplishments, but he was relentless, and the conversation spiraled downward. I kept looking at him and wondering: Why, if he had billions of dollars, did he feel the need to put me down? Certainly he had better things to do.

After twenty minutes, I smiled, thanked him, and wrapped up the meeting. Kalpana and I walked out of the room and one of the Barbies saw us out. As soon as the door closed behind us and the dry, hot Palo Alto air hit our faces, Kalpana turned to me and shook her head. "Screw him," she said with a smile. "I will invest in your company. Durreen, you are going to change the world, and I want to be at your side when you do it!"

I exhaled, smiled, and reached to give her a hug. My voice cracked with emotion as I thanked her. I had hoped that, with all of IIX's accomplishments, we would not have to go the friends-and-family route to get funding. The governing narrative of the financial system is that companies "grow out" of that need, and it's seen as a weakness to rely on friends and family for too long. But now, seeing the sparkle in Kalpana's eye, I understood that maybe I didn't need Silicon Valley on my side. Perhaps IIX simply needed to gather the right people on our team: people with a genuine desire to make a deep impact with capital and the rebellious, defiant spirit of undermining the system that had benefited them. Who needs venture capital firms, sitting on their clouds of billions of dollars, when you've got friends on the ground, ready to get to work to make real change happen?

CHAPTER TWENTY-EIGHT

Make Their Weapons Your Tools

Hosting conferences, producing research, lining up investors, measuring impact: we were expanding our impact ecosystem by the day. But it was still not enough. We had partnerships with some large banks and with companies like Bloomberg TV. Yet many of these companies boxed our work into their "corporate social responsibility" initiatives, which is essentially code for marketing that makes a company look like it's doing good.

We didn't have a problem with companies wanting to look good. But we needed them to walk the talk, too. We needed them to embrace changes that would make a real difference in the world.

We were chipping away at the system from the edges, but we still were far from taking the bull of Wall Street by the horns. To alter the financial system, worth over $120 trillion, we had to make people in positions of power sit up and take notice. We had created financing platforms and impact metrics, but we were still on the periphery of the action. We needed to penetrate the actual financial market. Like a matador waving a shimmering cape in front of a raging bull, we needed to tame the financial markets. At IIX we wanted to force inclusion to the core of the financial system, where it belongs. But how?

We were creating an impact investing ecosystem while channeling investments into a handful of companies, but if we were going to move the needle, we needed to bring more investment to more companies faster. We needed to create innovative financial solutions that would allow larger amounts of investments into these companies so that they can create a sustainable impact while reducing the investment risk. I knew what needed to happen, but I had no idea how to bring it all together.

The answer came to me one sunny afternoon as I watched Aliya ride a horse at the Equestrian Center in Singapore. There she was, wearing a cooling vest, to keep her body temperature stable, along with her jodhpurs and black helmet. She looked fashionable and yet so small on top of a massive white stallion, whose muscles rippled under his shiny coat.

I watched in awe as Aliya carefully controlled the powerful white horse's movements, making him trot, canter, turn, and go in all different directions. Standing at the fence, squinting my eyes to filter out the glaring tropical sun, I watched my daughter harness the animal's power and turn it into her power.

I had put Aliya in riding classes after reading about how children with physical and mental challenges often gain confidence by interacting with horses. Now I could see why. When you can't control your own body, working together with another powerful, living being can be healing. Building the courage to control something much stronger than yourself gives you inner power. In the process, you learn to tame your fears and take well-calculated risks.

The financial markets are extremely powerful, which is why they are often depicted as a raging bull. A bull, like a horse, ripples with might. I knew that now, having tried for years to tame the bull of the financial markets. But now I could see that I needed to be more like Aliya. I needed to do a better job of controlling the bull and the associated risks. I needed to use my skills to work more broadly and with more ease and grace.

I believed I could take away elements of risk and fear from people when they looked at my daughter, and I believed we could take away risk and fear for investors when they looked at an opportunity to create livelihoods for underserved women. But it would require nothing less than a revolution of inclusion: for my daughters, for women, for the underserved, and for the planet. We needed to value and treat all these voices as equals—and not out of pity or charity. Women and the underserved were not charity cases who needed handouts. They had solutions we needed to respect.

I kept thinking about how to make our impact enterprises appear less "risky" in the eyes of potential investors. I wracked my brain, thinking back through the history of finance in search of a precedent. Who else had successfully opened the financial market for new players? How had they done it?

As I brainstormed with Rob and our colleagues about how to use our power to unlock larger sources of capital for impact enterprises, one person's name kept coming up. Someone had already created a type of "risky" bond that had opened financial markets to companies that previously had not had access. There was one little problem, though. This person—the one I was beginning to think might hold the keys to unlocking our dilemma—was also a convicted felon.

***

Michael Milken became known in the 1980s as the King of Junk Bonds for having developed a financial instrument known as "high-yield bonds." In general, bonds are a way for a company to borrow money from a broad group of investors. First, a company issues a bond, investors buy the bond like they would any other investment, and then the company pays the investors back over time, with interest, as if the company had taken out a loan.

Milken's high-yield bonds were considered very risky, as they were issued by companies that had traditionally been ignored by the financial markets (which is why they came to be called "junk bonds": the companies were considered junk). Milken succeeded by reorienting investors' perceptions to think of the bonds as not only high risk but also high *return*, meaning that investors could be highly rewarded for taking the risk of buying these bonds. Milken was not the first person to issue high-yield bonds; they go back at least as far as the Massachusetts Bay Colony in the seventeenth century and were used by the first treasury secretary, Alexander Hamilton. Yet Milken structured this financial product in such a way that allowed contemporary companies that had previously been excluded from the mainstream financial markets (sometimes because of discrimination due to their owners' religious and economic backgrounds) to raise billions of dollars.

Eventually, companies began issuing high-yield bonds to raise money in order to acquire other companies. The power of this new financial instrument made Milken extremely wealthy. Unfortunately, he didn't know when to stop. Over time, he broke securities laws and ended up in prison. People in the financial world rightly condemn Milken's criminal acts, but they often still quietly admire his brilliance. And his innovation—high-yield bonds—have been a part of the mainstream ever since.

Once the idea of Milken's genius got into my head, I could not stop thinking about it. The question kept growing: How could we use this highly effective tool in our work? Were there other financial tools that had been put to unsavory use that we could repurpose for good?

I didn't have to think too hard. If you had to choose the greatest single contributor to the global financial crisis of 2008—the crisis which had led those of us at the Bellagio gathering to pioneer impact investing—it would be the collateralized loan obligation, or CLO. This tool had allowed Wall Street firms to repackage risky subprime mortgage loans as bonds.

These two highly effective yet dangerous instruments—high-yield bonds and CLOs—both tackled the notion of risk of an investment by diversifying it: one by pulling together a group of varied loans from individuals under one financial instrument and the other by sheer innovation of bond structuring for companies that could not otherwise enter the financial markets. Both had been used in the world of high finance to make lots of money for a small group of people.

But what if these tools could be used, with the right intentions and in a responsible way, to promote the common good? Nuclear weapons have killed millions—but the science behind nuclear technology eventually gave rise to zero-emissions energy and even new discoveries in medicine. Might there be a way to harness the immense power of these tools for the inclusion of all rather than the extreme wealth of a few?

***

One afternoon our team sat together in a conference room discussing how our impact enterprises kept coming back to us for more and more growth capital. They were still not being embraced by investors outside our private investment platform. As we debated the merits of continuing to support these enterprises, I grabbed the chance to share a bold idea with the group.

"We can't blame them for coming back," I insisted; "it's because the financial market for the impact we are creating is still nascent. The next stage of capital that these enterprises need from the market is just not there. In Asia, we are at the mercy of a few rich people—their funds and networks—who are fundamentally risk averse to investing in these companies. So how do we attract larger institutional investors from the traditional financial markets to invest?"

I paused and looked at our team, which was gathered around a table in the conference room, "We can't change a system if we are at the mercy of these few players!" I said. "We need to create a financial instrument that will truly connect the back streets of underserved communities with the Wall Streets of the world. That instrument is a bond. An innovative bond structure will take these enterprises directly to the formal financial market and its huge sums of capital."

I took a deep breath before naming the antihero whose brilliant product had led me to this thinking. "We need to do what Michael Milken did in the 1980s but in a more inclusive and creative—and legal—way."

I waited, wondering if our staff thought I was crazy. Rob took the bait. He knew how my mind worked. He was usually skeptical of my ideas at first, but he'd test them out and often eventually embrace them. "You know the impact companies we work with are tiny compared to most publicly listed companies," Rob said matter-of-factly.

"They can never go to the traditional financial market on their own. We tried the public market route. It was too difficult. Look at the public social stock exchange we launched in Mauritius; it's barely operating. The market is not open to these new things. I think we should just stick to operating our private placement platform and be happy with that."

"But let me show you," I said. I walked up to the whiteboard and started drawing the structure of a bond. "See, we would take flavors of the two brilliant 'evils' of the financial markets—Milken's junk bonds from the 1980s and the CLOs from the 2000s—and incorporate the most important component missing from the financial market: the participation of women."

Rob squinted. I had lost the others, but Rob was still with me. We shared an intellectually competitive spirit. After all these years together, we fed on challenges from each other. "So we pull together many enterprises in a group," I continued. "We make sure the group is diversified—with enterprises of different sizes, operating in a number of different countries, and in a range of sectors—but all focused on creating livelihoods for women. Then we issue a *single* bond, listed on a stock exchange, enabling the largest institutional investors to provide financing to all these enterprises who until now were shut out of the public financial markets, at once!"

I finished and stepped back from the whiteboard like an eager student showing off the solution to a complicated math problem. The team looked doubtful. Rob said he liked the structure of the bond as I had outlined it but that it would take months to pull together. We just didn't have the resources.

I disagreed. "We are at the cusp of something big here," I said. "Other people just create funds or take philanthropic funds and call it 'investment' when they provide a grant to an impact enterprise. What we are doing is the real deal, with the connection to the public financial market. It is not about a group of rich people putting a fund together and then dictating how economic development needs to happen; that's what I saw at the World Bank. Here we are celebrating and empowering the work at the ground level and then putting it into a high-finance structure and floating it in the public financial market for real institutional investors."

I was convinced that we were onto something. Through a bond we'd be creating a sturdier base of support for the impact enterprises that were quietly addressing climate change and inequality. The bond would reduce risk so that investors would have the confidence to invest in women.

***

As we shopped our proposal for the bond, which we had begun to call the Women's Livelihood Bond, to foundations and development banks, we received feedback: still too risky, maybe even impossible. These words always struck me as incongruous when they came from these organizations. Wasn't their job to take risks in service of a greater cause? Weren't they attempting the impossible every time they threw money at a problem to make change happen?

We had already proven that we could do the impossible. We had convinced investors—even Asian investors, some of the most conservative in the world—to invest in impact companies. We had created a system to measure impact in a form that investors could understand. We had proven with our impact measurement that the positive change created in the lives of employees, customers, and related beneficiaries and stakeholders—better health, education, and well-being—had ripple effects on the community. We had demonstrated how organizations with deep community impact were also less risky. Better environmental practices such as sustainable agriculture, careful water usage, and clean energy saved trees, nourished the soil, and made the water supply healthy, and the healthier the environment and resources in the community are, the healthier the business's odds of success. At IIX, we were supporting businesses in which women were leading the way on these local changes toward more sustainable practices, making decisions such as switching to clean cookstoves, growing their own vegetables, or cultivating fish for food security.

By this point in 2015, traditional financial markets at last had begun showing interest in sustainability. This was partly due to the newly minted United Nations Sustainable Development Goals (the SDGs, now more commonly known as the Global Goals). Seventeen interlocking global goals, developed by the member nations of the UN, focused on achieving a more sustainable future for the planet and its people. The goals covered hunger alleviation, poverty reduction, health, water, clean energy, gender equality, responsible consumption, climate action, sustainable oceans, peace, and partnership.

When the SDGs started gaining momentum in global conversations, our team at IIX felt relieved, given the clear alignment between the SDGs and our work. Our mission was becoming mainstream. The SDGs explicitly called on the private sector to contribute to achieving these goals by 2030—and we were thrilled to play a role in this effort.

Before long, the Rockefeller Foundation, which had helped us launch IIX, came through with half the money we needed to develop the bond. With that, we pulled together a small team, headed by Rob, which began work on structuring the bond.

To create the bond, we first needed to select a group of impact enterprises to include in the bond portfolio. We were looking for a special group: ones that created sustainable livelihoods for women through their work and met our stringent impact assessment standards but that also had financial histories solid enough to satisfy investors and the stock market's regulations. Once we had all of these components, we could create a bond to fund these companies and list it on a stock exchange.

As we searched for women-centered organizations that fit this bill, I remembered the Filipino enterprise that had been a former supplier to oneNest. A drop in global sugar prices had devastated the sugar plantation-driven economy of the Negros Occidental region, resulting in widespread famine; oneNest had lifted thousands of women and their families out of hunger by selling their handmade household items through this enterprise, such as embroidered photo frames, jewelry boxes, and tablemats.

Could we now bring women from remote villages of the Philippines to the financial markets? The world should know how these women had persevered. They had worked so hard to pull themselves from the clutches of a devastating famine, and they had survived and even prospered. Now we believed they were ready to debut in the international financial markets. I reached out to the CEO of the enterprise, reintroducing myself and asking whether they wanted to be part of this innovative financial structure for the women of their cooperative.

Within hours, we had received a positive response. Yes, they could use the funds that the Women's Livelihood Bond would provide to expand their operations and reach more than 50,000 women. I smiled when I read the note. All the pieces were falling into place.

CHAPTER TWENTY-NINE

Be Inspired by Those
Who Went Before

The second-floor window of the mosque opened onto a shimmering lake surrounded by trees. Banyan, mango, albizia, and krishnochura trees shaded the banks of the lake, lending a bit of tranquility to the bustling city. The mosque, with its high arching domes and spacious prayer rooms covered in colorful prayer rugs, was just a few blocks from our family house in Dhaka, Bangladesh. Dadu and a group of his friends had begun construction on the mosque during my childhood. Even before its completion, the mosque served as a community center for prayers and for the needy. Bubu would regularly send food and fruits from our trees to the mosque, to be distributed to the hungry.

Standing in the women's section of that mosque now, wearing a white shalwar kameez with a white dupatta covering my head, I was surrounded by my sisters, female cousins, and hundreds of other women.

The occasion was my mother's funeral. I was numb. Thousands of people had come, and I saw many familiar faces. All of us were quietly crying after finishing our prayers. We watched from the second-floor windows as thousands of men, gathered on the massive grounds surrounding the mosque, said the last rite prayers in front of the body, which lay on a simple wooden structure covered in a white shroud.

Funeral prayers had to be held outside of the mosque because there were so many mourners. Women behind me were whispering that the mosque had never seen so many mourners in its history. Men spilled out of the mosque grounds and onto the road. They sat on their prayer mats on the ground, wiping their tears while saying their *namaz* for the deceased.

My thoughts drifted back to the last time I had seen my mother alive. She was lying on the divan in excruciating pain from a broken hip but still, somehow, with a serene smile on her face. All her children had flown in from around the world to be with her. She kept on joking that it had taken her broken hip to bring us together after all these years. We were all trying to convince her to have an operation, but she adamantly refused.

I was alone in the room with her, leaning against the bookshelf bursting with hundreds of the romances Ma used to devour in her forties. Reading romances was Ma's escape. I could never understand why all the heroines in these romance novels acted so helpless or what about them appealed to my mother.

"Ma, do you need anything? Do you need some more painkillers? Do you want something to drink?" I needed to do something.

Ma smiled. She patted the divan indicating for me to sit next to her. "I want you to know something," Ma said softly. "I want you to know I am happy that you never listened to me." The gentle smile was still on her face. How could she look so beautiful even when she was in so much pain? Her sari was still perfectly draped, her hair braided with the plait falling gently over her shoulder. Her big expressive eyes were glassy with tears, but there was a strange joy in them.

I was startled. What did she mean? I knew how much grief she had received after she gave birth to me, the fourth daughter. Then as I grew up I had been so angry at our culture, and I had given her a hard time. "I am sorry I was such a rebel," I told her, tears rolling down my cheeks.

"But you were *my* rebel, and it's your rebellious passion that is changing the world," she said. "I am so very proud of you. I am glad you did not listen to me or anyone but did what you felt was right."

Now, watching her body being carried by mourners, I felt a massive ball of grief and regret and anger settling into my stomach. My mother had helped countless people during her lifetime. Yes, she had been a product of her culture. But she had also been a feminist in her own way, pushing the boundaries of a restrictive society and religion. She had raised five children and had put her four daughters through Catholic school. She believed in the work that the nuns were doing and the education they were providing to us and to the children in the slums surrounding the school. She had also educated and provided for hundreds of girls in the orphanages and had made sure we had a bond with those children. She had empowered women who were destitute to find a better life by teaching them cooking and sewing and helping them find work. She had helped dozens of men get small businesses off the ground, making each of them feel valued as she advised them and spoke to them in their local dialect. Her only condition? That those men promise to educate their daughters. She had been a defiant optimist.

Now that same woman was covered head to toe in a white shroud, surrounded by praying men. As is the custom, only men are allowed to participate in the Islamic funeral rite. Women are not allowed to take part even when the deceased is a woman. It's as though women can't go to the afterlife without the help of men. I was changing a financial system to include women, but I could not change the rituals of a religion to say goodbye to my mother up close.

I watched men put the wooden structure in the back of a truck. Our dead are transported from the mosque to the graveyard without any pomp or grandeur. Watching out the window, I could smell perfume in the air. Was it *attar*, the rose oil used at religious gatherings, or the sandalwood incense from the funeral? No, it smelled like French perfume that my mother loved. I closed my eyes and took a deep breath. The fragrance likely came from a woman nearby, maybe even someone who wore it in memory of my mother. Still, the aroma made me feel like my mother was there with me.

Looking out the window, I pledged to her that I would finish the work that she had started. I would do it for her, for Bubu, for my sisters, for my daughters, and for all the women cordoned off from living their fullest lives by systems that exclude them.

***

Ma's death wrapped a blanket of sadness around me, but it also made me reflect on my daughters. The girls were trying to absorb what the death of their grandmother—a strong figure in their lives—meant for them. They needed to make *Amma* proud by becoming independent and strong women.

Every night before they went to bed, I asked them to tell me three things: what made them sad that day, what made them happy, and what they loved about themselves. Sometimes they'd say, in answer to the last question, "Everything." When you are the parent of a girl and hear that answer, you smile.

Ma's death also energized me in a strange way, making me even more determined to complete our financial innovation: the Women's Livelihood Bond. By now, we had assembled a powerhouse team to bring the bond to life. Angela—our COO, a former accountant, and a UN veteran—was picking up the pieces of running the company. Natasha, with a hedge fund background, worked with Rob on the bond mechanics and kept all the partners across the region working together: bankers, accountants, and law firms.

We were still missing one piece: a way to "derisk" the bond. We needed a concrete measure to make the bond seem less risky to investors. The diversification of the bond's portfolio—which included a variety of enterprises, across different industries, from a number of countries—helped. But investors still wanted some sort of insurance policy so that if something went wrong, their investment would be protected. In the financial world, this usually comes in the form of a guarantee: a promise on the part of certain investors to take on more risk. In return for higher returns, those investors would be the first ones to take a hit, protecting other investors in the event of losses.

I spoke to countless foundations and government development agencies that often backed bonds with a guarantee, but even for them, our bond was too funky. They had never seen such financial structures.

Even as I was combing my brain for strategies to get at least one of these donors to back our work, private-sector partners started signing up with us with vigor. It was amazing. They wanted to find a way to show their support for the United Nations' Sustainable Development Goals, and working with IIX was the perfect way to do it. We had global law firms and large banks from across the region rolling up their sleeves to be part of this groundbreaking initiative—all pro bono. Without compensation, the law firms worked with us to draft documentation for the bond, while the banks advised us on outreach to potential investors.

Just when I thought we had turned over all the stones in the search for a guarantor, I received a note from a business acquaintance, Kevin Martin. He was an enthusiastic supporter of our work at the United States Agency for International Development (USAID). USAID leads the US government's response to international development and disaster, and it administers grants to partners around the world. Kevin was an enthusiastic supporter of our work. A few months earlier, he had been almost as disappointed as we had been when USAID rejected our request for financial support for the Women's Livelihood Bond. The money we had applied for, which had been earmarked for gender-lens investing in Asia, had gone instead to a consulting firm based in the United States. The firm—which had no experience in finance, investing in women or Asia—received the funding to write a paper on the topic. The fact that this funding had gone to them rather than to us was still difficult for me to swallow.

"Durreen," Kevin was saying now on the phone, "I actually think we can help you derisk the bond!" I could hear the excitement in Kevin's voice, a deviation from his usual lawyerly manner.

"I think your relentless calls to various governments finally did the trick," he continued. "My colleagues and I met with the development arm of the Australian government at a conference. The Australians are intrigued by the bond, but they didn't have the right tools to help you. We have the tools but not the budget. So we agreed to work together to provide a guarantee for the Women's Livelihood Bond!"

I was thrilled to hear Kevin's news. To see how two governments— the United States and Australia—were collaborating to support women's representation in the public financial market made me ecstatic. This was a new way of changing the world directly, led by the people of the Global South through the financial markets.

"Now let's get the guarantee sorted out and get this bond to the market," Kevin said. It felt like we were back on track and nearing the finish line of this race to closing the Women's Livelihood Bond.

Sometimes when we get within a few steps of a finish line, however, it seems to shift once again. As often happens when you are a woman working to change deeply embedded practices in society, the closer you get to the endpoint, the farther away that endpoint seems to move.

CHAPTER THIRTY

Stay True to the Vision

We were in the IIX conference room, in our weekly "all hands" conference call, when it all broke open. In this call all the bankers and lawyers, working across the various countries and time zones, came together to comb through the tangles of the bond: structuring, legal issues, financial implications. We had completed our financial and social reviews and selected three enterprises to support with the proceeds we would raise from the sale of the bond. One enterprise in Vietnam focused on improving the lives of women factory workers. One in Cambodia provided small loans to rural women. And the Filipino enterprise offered microfinancing for women entrepreneurs in the Philippines.

We were almost there. The bond was structured. The guarantee was in place. The enterprises were ready. The expected impact on women's livelihoods had been assessed. We were ready to sell the bond and list it on Singapore's stock exchange, one of the largest and most respected stock exchanges in the world. We wanted this bond to be listed in a traditional exchange and not our own exchange to ensure that the bond would usher impact investing into a formal, global, financial phenomenon. Nothing like this had ever happened before: a bond *for* women, *by* women (and a few good men), being listed on a global public stock exchange.

Only one problem remained: finding enough investors. We and the banking partners were pounding the pavement, but somehow we could not move the needle. Investors liked the idea of the bond, but they were not willing to commit. Sometimes Rob joined us on our sales calls. He really didn't like the selling aspect of our work, but as a white man and recent investment banker, he often served as a great "derisker" in the eyes of the market. Usually, when Rob got involved, investors would come in with an investment. But in the case of the Women's Livelihood Bond, even the white-man quotient was not working. We could not understand what was happening.

Finally, on the conference call that day, we got our answer when one of the bankers said the quiet part out loud. "We can't sell this bond because of the perceived risk," he said.

Rob jumped in, frustrated. "You know how far we have gone to minimize risk for investors. We've selected a diversified group of enterprises with strong credit profiles. And we have a guarantee from the US and Australian governments. What else do investors need?"

"I'm just telling you that this is what the market thinks," he said. "We can't change the market sentiment!"

The banker paused. "But there *is* one thing we thought of that you could do to change the risk perception," he said. "You could change the name of the bond from 'Women's Livelihood Bond' to something else. Maybe call it simply a 'High-Yield Emerging Market Bond.' Now *that* we could sell!"

On the phone, the banker couldn't see the incredulous look that was surely spreading over my face. He added bluntly, "Let's face it: 'Women's Livelihood' does sound very risky and 'nonprofit-y.'"

His words landed with a thud. A rare moment of silence enveloped all the high-powered people on the call. I felt the attention of everyone pointing toward me.

Suddenly I felt tired. So tired. I was tired of bending over backward to make everything fit the male psyche, tired of making everything run according to the male version of finance. The whole point of doing this bond was to connect women to capital: to bend the financial market toward them, and improve the livelihoods of women, their communities, and our planet. And now we were being told to scrub the very identity of the bond from its name? To hide the very nature and mission of our work?

No. "That is not even a remote possibility," I said. "I will never—and I emphasize *never*—change the name of the bond. Otherwise, what was the point of all this?" I gestured around the room. My voice came out on a high pitch of anger.

There was more silence on the call. Rob, Natasha, the rest of the team, and I watched the silent speakerphone in the center of our conference table.

"Hello? Is everyone still there?" I inquired.

"Fine," the banker eventually said. "If you won't change the name, you'll need to bring in an additional layer of investment to act as a 'first loss' to protect the bond investors." There was a bit more chilly silence before he added, "Once you've found that, we can talk. Until then, I am afraid we are all wasting our time."

One by one, all the callers dropped off. We sat around the table, staring at each other. The banker was suggesting that we find an investor who would agree to be paid back only after the other investors were all paid back. In effect, that investor would be agreeing to absorb any losses—the "first loss"—up to the amount of their investment, before the bondholders would have to accept any loss. This would be the cushion even before the guarantee kicks in.

First-loss investment would be much riskier than an investment in the bond itself—which, we were being told, was *already* too risky for investors. Who could we find to invest in that?

I was speechless. "I can't believe it," I said finally. "I can't believe it will all come crashing down now, at the last minute, after years of work!"

Fighting the system seemed endless. We had all sacrificed so much for this company, for this bond, for the women out there who just needed a bridge to gain respect and credit and capital. We had almost finished building this bridge for them, but now it looked like we wouldn't be able to finish the last few feet. I saw no way forward. I rested my head on folded arms, trying hard to fight back tears.

"Everyone, can you please give Durreen and me a few minutes?" Rob requested quietly. I heard the glass door open and close.

"Bahu, we need to do this. We need to do this for the girls," he said. "We need to do this for my mother and yours. We need to do this for the millions of women out there. Remember when you gave me that big speech convincing me to join IIX?"

It was true. When I had invited him to join IIX for no salary, I had really laid it on thick: the idealism, the defiance, the belief that we could change how financial systems treat women in underserved communities. "Well, now is my turn to give you that same speech," he said. "We cannot give up now."

Rob paused. I still had my head down. I could not face him. This man had sacrificed his own career for my dreams of changing the world. And now I had let him down right at the finish line.

"Bahu, I think we should put in our savings for the first loss," he said softly. "If we put in our own money as a backup, then investors will rally around this bond."

I lifted my head to look at Rob. He looked tired but determined. We couldn't do that, I protested, first in my head and then out loud to Rob. We had already put too much into this company. We had gone without salaries for years, and what Rob was proposing would mean risking the last bit of financial security we had. Our savings were for the girls, and we couldn't afford to put their future education and well-being on the line. We simply couldn't use it for the first loss. Yes, if the bond worked we would get paid back. But if the bond didn't work, then we would, put simply, lose everything. And I wouldn't be able to live with that.

I kept shaking my head no. But I was also amazed at the all-in gamble he was proposing. My husband felt so passionately about our bond that he was willing to risk everything for it?

"We have no choice," he said. "We have to do it. The bond will work. I know it. Trust me on this. If we put in the money, I know it will sell." Rob kept pushing. He was clearly not going to give up.

"Rob, are you sure?" I could not get my head around the terrifying thing that was happening. Yet something was also beginning to spark inside me. The chill I had felt just moments earlier was replaced by a warm glow somewhere in my stomach.

"We can't give up now," he said. "If we do, we lose all of the work we have put into this. It will all be OK. Let's tell the bankers and lawyers now." He reached out and squeezed my hand. I nodded.

It was decided. He pushed his chair back and went out to share the decision with the team. Within hours, we had let everyone know that the bond was back on track.

**

With the first loss in place, the Women's Livelihood Bond sold in a matter of days. It became the world's first gender-lens impact investing security to be listed on a stock exchange.

When everything was done, Angela, Natasha, Rob, and I watched the Women's Livelihood Bond displayed for the first time on the Bloomberg terminal, that hallowed symbol of Wall Street's power. The Bloomberg listing showed all the details of the Women's Livelihood Bond. Its ticker, its principal amount (the amount we had raised), and its coupon (the interest rate we promised to pay investors). The screen had numbers and graphs on it, filled with fascinating data, but my eyes glazed over. All I could see were the smiles of thousands of women who would benefit from the bond.

We were creating history. We were reinventing finance to make it work for the 99 percent—specifically for women in the remotest parts of Southeast Asia who now had access to financial markets through our livelihood bond.

The first Women's Livelihood Bond would eventually raise $8.5 million and would improve the lives of 385,000 women over four years. It gave them access to credit and improved their livelihoods. By the end of the first year, it had impacted 144,800 women, far more than we had estimated.

By the end of 2022, we had issued a total of five Women's Livelihood Bonds in the market. That first one that we struggled so hard to bring to fruition has been completely paid off, and the others continue to make regular payments to their investors from across the globe even during the height of the pandemic. We have funneled more than $300 million into impact enterprises across fifty-three countries, and we've supported millions of women running small businesses in the last mile. By creating the world's first bond focused on women to be listed on a stock exchange, we proved that valuing women, underserved communities, and the planet can be a part of the financial system which, until a few years ago, worked for just the 1 percent.

I stared at the Bloomberg listing tick by. I thought of defiant, optimistic women like Melinda, in the Philippines, who started borrowing from a cooperative that is a part of the bond in 2000 with an initial loan of fifty dollars. At that time, she was supporting her family of five children by selling fish and bananas. She started accumulating savings in order to set up her own pig farm. Now, thanks to the Women's Livelihood Bond, Melinda could obtain a larger loan to grow her small farm. Her increased income and savings allowed her to pay for her children's tuition fees and school allowances and eventually send all her children to college.

I think of Bopha, a smallholder organic farmer in Cambodia. Her shiny, smiling eyes peek out from the shade under the wicker farmer's hat she wears. An organic rice enterprise in Cambodia that is part of the Women's Livelihood Bond Series buys rice from Bopha. With financing from the bond, the enterprise helped Bopha receive training on organic and sustainable rice farming, which in turn helped her increase her yield per harvest by 20 percent. Through the Women's Livelihood Bond, Bopha now belongs to the greater financial markets: markets that now work for her.

Agni, a woman in Indonesia, comes to mind. At first glance, she may appear shy and timid but a few minutes of conversation reveal to you the defiant look in her eyes, the smile of determination. Agni borrowed small loans from an Indonesian cooperative offering microfinance services to its members. The most recent loan Agni took allowed her to buy water filters, saving two hours a day collecting water from other locations. Access to clean water has improved her family's overall health and increased her total income by allowing her to spend her additional hours in the day at her small store. Now Agni is linked to the financial market.

There are more than a million Melindas, Bophas, and Agnis in our bonds, spread all across South Asia, Southeast Asia, and Africa. They are the real defiant optimists, I thought, as I watched the Bloomberg listing unfurl in front of us—the women who, like my mother, did not accept the role that society laid out for them. Now they were proudly part of the global financial markets.

As I took in the reality of the Singapore Stock Exchange and Bloomberg listing, I thought of Bubu, and Ma, and Rokeya, and Amina, and the women of Bangladesh who were harmed in the war of independence but refused to be cowed. I thought of the women in saris on their motorbikes in India, racing past us on their way to their tailor shop or store or salon, and women in underserved communities around the globe whose enterprising spirits were improving the lives of their neighbors and the health of the planet. I thought of my sisters, my nieces, and now my daughters, Diya and Aliya. I thought of my students, all our partners, my IIX team members, and all the other women and men who had shared their defiance and optimism and skills and passion.

A few years after the first Women's Livelihood Bond launched, I was invited to speak to the United Nations General Assembly about using finance as a source of power and peace. Wearing my red nakshi kantha sari, stitched lovingly by women in Bangladesh, I told leaders from around the world about how we can reshape finance to work for the 99 percent.

The day of my speech at the UN happened to be my fiftieth birthday—the very day on which, every year, my grandfather would tell me about the portentous moment of my birth. I shared with my audience at the UN my grandfather's words: about how this moment—chura moni—came only once in a century and about the way he would shake his head. The promise of that rare moment, chura moni—the peak, the jewel—could only be reached by a male child. "If only you had been a boy, then you could have reached great heights," he would say. I told them how I always hoped his interpretation of chura moni would someday include me in a future vision of great heights, but it never had.

Standing in front of the UN General Assembly, I realized that I was no longer ashamed of my birthday. Millions of women gave me the courage to be proud. Women like Melinda, Bopha, Agni, and Priya have become my chura moni: my peak and my jewel. They are creating a world where all of us belong.

Defying countless obstacles, we keep pushing. Living with systems designed to keep some in and some out, we find the courage to keep fighting. We become pragmatic in the face of tough decisions. We defy fate and refuse to believe it is our future, and we look with hope toward what is to come. We seize the opportunity to provide a better life for ourselves, our families, our communities, and our planet. We defy the systems that keep people out, and we hold out hope that change is possible: defiantly, optimistically, together.

Commitments of the Defiant Optimist

Defiant optimists work toward a world of inclusion, opportunity, and sharing of power. Defiant optimism is not only about empowering yourself; it is about empowering countless others who don't have the means to stand up to the system. You can be a defiant optimist no matter what realm of work you inhabit.

As Defiant Optimists, we:

➤ Dare to imagine a better world and improve the lives of those around us, whether in our local community or on a global scale.

➤ Stay pragmatic about achieving a goal that is for the greater good, even if it takes countless tries to get there.

➤ Demand respect. We respect ourselves and claim respect for others who cannot gain it for themselves. If someone respects you, they give you power; that becomes power within you, and you become empowered to take action.

➤ Ask ourselves: Who else will we fail if we can't push forward?

➤ Refuse to take no for an answer. A no is never really a no. Dig hard enough to find that morsel of information that may turn a no into a yes.

➤ Believe in ourselves and command the attention of others. We must be loud, angry, and determined, and we must focus our effort on what we know is right.

➤ Create our own village. Seek out like-minded people, build alliances with them, and embrace their assistance. We need champions on our side to change the course of an organization and system.

➤ Be generous without expecting returns. In life, return and value comes in many different ways, shapes, and forms.

➤ Remold the structures around us to make them more inclusive. Courage demands we be willing to work hard for this change.

➤ Acknowledge the personal qualities and wins that brought us here.

➤ Share our power and opportunities with others to empower them.

Acknowledgments

Although I wrote the initial words of this book, a village came together to bring it to life. My heartfelt thanks and gratitude to all listed here for their unwavering support, encouragement, guidance, and love.

My acquisitions editor at Broadleaf Books, Valerie Weaver-Zercher: thank you for your encouragement, suggestions, tireless edits, and, most importantly, for making a writer out of me.

My personal editor, Diana McKeage: thank you for being my writing partner, guide, and "daughter from another life" all wrapped in one. This book wouldn't have seen the light of day without you there next to me.

My friends and supporters: Elana Abraham for being my rock; Deepa Chatrath for being my spiritual compass; Judith Asphar for being my guardian angel; Edward Hartman for being my writing muse; Mukul Panday for being an unwavering supporter; Gill Saul for showing me the link between art and words; and Kalpana Raina and Rory Riggs for believing in me from hello.

Annie Chang and the RS Foundation: thank you for the funding support that allowed me to devote time and resources to the early work on this book.

My parents, maternal grandparents, and siblings: thank you for pointing me toward the north star of social justice. Chachu, thank you for always lovingly defending my defiance.

My wise, understanding daughters, Diya and Aliya: thank you for making me want to be a better person every day.

My ever-patient, loving, and supportive husband and life partner, Robert Kraybill: "I am because we are." Thank you for your unwavering belief in me and for encouraging me to live life according to my terms.

My IIX colleagues: thank you for believing in our work. Thank you also for your wonderful suggestions along my writing journey.

This book would have had a very different ending without IIX's volunteers, staff, advisors, partners, and stakeholders over the past thirteen years. Thank you to those in the book, and the many others whose stories could not be included—many more than I can name here.

Thank you to those who provided early support to IIX, including the Rockefeller Foundation, the Department of Foreign Affairs and Trade of Australia, the US International Development Finance Corporation, USAID, and a number of other development and government agencies, including KOICA, P4G, UNESCAP, UNCDF, and the Monetary Authority of Singapore, who provided support in the years leading up to the development of the Women's Livelihood Bond Series. Thank you to our private-sector partners who volunteered their time to help my vision of the Women's Livelihood Bond come to life. Thank you, Shearman & Sterling, Latham & Watkins, Clifford Chance, Cyril Amarchand Mangaldas, ANZ Bank, Standard Chartered Bank, Barclays Bank, and DBS Bank.

Thank you to my former students and dozens of volunteers who helped write the business plan for IIX and who brought so much energy to IIX in its early days.

And to the millions of women across the globe who now belong to the financial system through IIX's work, welcome—and thank you for showing the rest of us how to be defiant optimists. Thank you for proving that we can connect the back streets of underserved communities to the Wall Streets of the world. Together we are creating our own nakshi kanthas of inclusion through defiant optimism.

Notes

PREFACE

The top 1 percent of households: "Top 1 Percent of Households Own 43 Percent of Global Wealth," TRT World, December 7, 2020, https://www.trtworld.com/magazine/top-1-percent-of-households-own-43-percent-of-global-wealth-42134.

more wealth than 4.6 billion people: "Time to Care: Unpaid and Underpaid Care Work and the Global Inequality Crisis," Oxfam Briefing Paper, January 2020, https://oxfamilibrary.openrepository.com/bitstream/handle/10546/620928/bp-time-to-care-inequality-200120-en.pdf.

each dollar that men earn: "Equal Pay for Work of Equal Value," UN Women, accessed April 26, 2022, https://www.unwomen.org/en/news/in-focus/csw61/equal-pay.

CHAPTER 1

due to sex-selective abortions: Ravinder Kaur and Taanya Kapoor, "The Gendered Biopolitics of Sex Selection in India," *Asian Bioethics Review* 13, no. 1 (2021): 111–27.

one in five are younger than fifteen: "Child Marriage," UNICEF, accessed July 19, 2022, https://www.unicef.org/rosa/what-we-do/child-protection/child-marriage.

CHAPTER 2

"Sexual violence is deployed as a weapon": Kirthi Jayakumar, "Why Is Sexual Violence So Common in War?" *Peace Insight*, May 20, 2013, https://www.peaceinsight.org/en/articles/why-is-sexual-violence-so-common-in-war/?location=&theme=women-peace-security.

The UN now considers sexual violence: United Nations Security Council Resolution 1820, June 19, 2008, https://www.securitycouncilreport.org/atf/cf/%7B65BFCF9B-6D27-4E9C-8CD3-CF6E4FF96FF9%7D/CAC%20S%20RES%201820.pdf.

CHAPTER 14

one out of five women: Rahman, Nilufar, "Bangladesh Government Literacy Initiative: The Integrated Non Formal Education Program," Women Reading the World: Policies and Practices of Literacy in Asia, UNESCO Institute for Education, 1996, https://unesdoc.unesco.org/ark:/48223/pf0000113584.

women of color continue to receive: Emma Hinchliffe, "The Number of Black Female Founders Who Have Raised More than $1 Million Has Nearly Tripled Since 2018," *Fortune*, December 2, 2020, https://fortune.com/2020/12/02/black-women-female-founders-venture-capital-funding-vc-2020-project-diane/.

CHAPTER 20

10 percent of female entrepreneurs: Bossoutrot Sylvie, "Gender Equality: Why It Matters, Especially in a Time of Crisis," World Bank, April 13, 2020, https://www.worldbank.org/en/news/opinion/2020/04/13/gender-equality-why-it-matters-especially-in-a-time-of-crisis.

CHAPTER 21

40 percent increase in diabetes: "Soft Drinks Could Increase Type 2 Diabetes Risk by 40 Per Cent," Diabetes.co.uk, February 27, 2010, https://www.diabetes.co.uk/news/2010/feb/soft-drinks-could-increase-type-2-diabetes-risk-by-40-per-cent-92661852.html.

80 percent of people displaced: "Climate Change Exacerbates Violence against Women and Girls," United Nations Human Rights Office of the High Commissioner, July 12, 2022, https://www.ohchr.org/en/stories/2022/07/climate-change-exacerbates-violence-against-women-and-girls; "Rapid, Climate-Informed Development Needed," World Bank, November 8, 2015, https://www.worldbank.org/en/news/feature/2015/11/08/rapid-climate-informed-development-needed-to-keep-climate-change-from-pushing-more-than-100-million-people-into-poverty-by-2030.

CHAPTER 22

Blended Value Map: Jed Emerson, "The Blended Value Map," William and Flora Hewlett Foundation, October 6, 2003, https://hewlett.org/library /the-blended-value-map-full-text/.

CHAPTER 23

wealthiest 10 percent of Americans: Robert Frank, "The Wealthiest 10% of Americans Own a Record 89% of All U.S. Stocks," CNBC, October 18, 2021, https://www.cnbc.com/2021/10/18/the-wealthiest-10percent-of-americans -own-a-record-89percent-of-all-us-stocks.html#:~:text=The%20wealth iest%2010%25%20of%20American,data%20from%20the%20Federal%20 Reserve.